With Aloha,
Bonnie Lee Mahler

Embrace the Moment

Bonnie Lee Mahler

BALBOA.
PRESS

A DIVISION OF HAY HOUSE

Balboa Press books may be ordered through booksellers or by contacting:

Balboa Press
A Division of Hay House
1663 Liberty Drive
Bloomington, IN 47403
www.balboapress.com
1 (877) 407-4847

Because of the dynamic nature of the Internet, any web addresses or
links contained in this book may have changed since publication and
may no longer be valid. The views expressed in this work are solely those
of the author and do not necessarily reflect the views of the publisher,
and the publisher hereby disclaims any responsibility for them.

The author of this book does not dispense medical advice or prescribe the use
of any technique as a form of treatment for physical, emotional, or medical
problems without the advice of a physician, either directly or indirectly. The
intent of the author is only to offer information of a general nature to help
you in your quest for emotional and spiritual well-being. In the event you use
any of the information in this book for yourself, which is your constitutional
right, the author and the publisher assume no responsibility for your actions.

Any people depicted in stock imagery provided by Thinkstock are models,
and such images are being used for illustrative purposes only.
Certain stock imagery © Thinkstock.

Printed in the United States of America.

ISBN: 978-1-5043-2534-9 (sc)
ISBN: 978-1-5043-2536-3 (hc)
ISBN: 978-1-5043-2535-6 (e)
Library of Congress Control Number: 2014922501

Balboa Press rev. date: 01/21/2015

Dedicated with lots of love to my three sons,
Tyler John, Trevor Chase, and Trenton Boyd

CONTENTS

ACKNOWLEDGMENTS

I have deep gratitude and appreciation for a life that is and has been so richly blessed by being surrounded by the most amazing people.

I am so thankful to family, friends, colleagues, and clients who have crossed my path and touched my life in their own unique ways. Each one has contributed to my experience and exploration of life. I know that without my connection with them, challenging or joyful, I would never have learned the lessons that were mine to learn. I offer my thanks to the following people:

My husband, Mark, the love of my life, for his wonderful family and the many exciting experiences he has brought to my journey. His unconditional love allows me to be who I am. His encouragement and support for me in writing this book have been constant.

My mother, El Marie Gunnell, who has been my mentor, teacher, and inspiration!

My father, William Paul Hansen, who lived his life with enthusiasm and a positive outlook.

My sons Tyler John and Trevor Chase, who gave their physical lives so that I could learn the lessons of sacrifice, compassion, courage, and many more.

My son Trenton Boyd, who continues to live his life as an example of faith, courage, and compassion, and with enthusiasm in everything that he does.

My sister Melody, has been my cheerleader. She is an example of determination and courage to me.

My sister Kathy has always been there for me with unconditional love and support. She is a great example of service and compassion.

My extended family, half brothers and half sisters Shelly Smith, Kelly Mease, Joe Hansen, and Bill Hansen, for our special relationships that have developed over the years.

Alan and Carol Coombs, the owners of Green Valley Spa and Resort in St. George, Utah, as well as their family and staff. For more than twenty years, Green Valley was a place for me to heal in times of need, and it provided an amazing place to practice what I loved: fitness and wellness.

My special friend Cindy Olsen Pulsipher, for the constant love, support, and encouragement of everything that I wanted to undertake. She is always there cheering me on, no matter what!

Trish and Lloyd Mecham, for their loving encouragement and support and for the many hours of voice coaching, training, and recording music. They believed in the talent that I had to share.

Zhane Hormechea—it was because of her that I had the opportunity to meet Celine Dion. Zhane has become a great friend and was very instrumental in providing me with the best Celine wig ever!

Holly Wilkinson, Bridget Merrell, and Tamera Sherman, for their continued friendship and the expertise that they brought to my Celine act.

Boyd Luke, a wonderful father to our sons, and one of my greatest teachers.

The creators of Impact Training Company, Sally and Hans Berger and their amazing trainers and staff.

Anna Erquiza Warlick, for our new friendship and the time and effort in assisting me with the huge task of organizing and the first editing of this book. A big *mahalo*!

Judy Fleming and Lindsey Pelliccia, great friends who believed that others deserved to hear my story, for their encouragement to get it done!

INTRODUCTION

I was raised in a positive environment. My parents always encouraged me to try things that I was afraid of. I learned early on not to tell my father that I was afraid of something, because inevitably he would advise me to face my fears. He would say, "If you are afraid of something, it is because you don't understand it or haven't experienced it. By experiencing it, your fear will disappear. Until we experience something, we cannot judge it. Leave your comfort zone. That is how you grow. That is how you build character!"

Growing up, I realized how much I loved and enjoyed being around people. Human behavior fascinates me. People continually teach me so much. I watch, listen, and take note of the lives that others create for themselves. I see the things that I don't want to create for myself as well as the things that I do. I look at others as my greatest teachers. I have always wanted to be an inspiration to others. I believe that through our examples we can influence others more than in any other way.

We each have a story; each is unique because we are all unique. We get to create our own paths. They are our roads and our journeys, paths that we create to learn from. Others come into our lives to walk with us, but no one can walk it for us. I didn't realize when I started my journey that in order to inspire others there would be events in my life and I would have to choose how I handled them. I had several impactful and challenging events that led me and prepared me to cope with the tragedy of losing my two eldest sons, in the space of two years. My two amazing sons had come into my life for a few brief moments in time so that I could experience what they had to teach me. I honor them for giving their physical lives so that I could grow and learn the many things that I did. This was the time to go deep within my heart and soul and take from this experience the strength and courage to move forward in creating positive things.

It was through the process of healing that I gained an understanding of what my purpose truly was. I realized that nothing just happens and that everything has a purpose. As part of my journey, I choose to go forward with a positive attitude of growth and learning. I want to share my story and inspire others toward hope and a belief that out of tragedy can come some of the greatest blessings and insight into the meaning of life. It can be so easy to become a victim or have a "poor me" attitude, but it was through my experiences of tragedy that I was able to bring forth amazing things in my own life. I gained understanding of how powerful I truly am—and the importance of free will to create my own reality. My wish is to inspire you to discover your own power within and to take that power and use it to create anything that you desire. In doing so, you influence others to do the same.

SECTION 1

HONOR THE PAST

CHAPTER 1

Be the change that you wish to see in the world.
—Unknown

So, here I am on Korean Airlines, flying over the Pacific Ocean on my way to Bali, Indonesia, a place I have only read about in travel magazines and brochures and have seen in the movies. I hear it is a worthy destination, a magical and beautiful retreat, with much culture to experience. Life is an adventure, and I am living another one! I had planned this trip for a year with my friends and have so looked forward to it. Bali is on the other side of the world from where we live and across the international date line. It will be a long, eighteen-hour trip: lots of time to read about the ultimate destination.

Bali is one of seventeen thousand islands that make up the country of Indonesia; eleven thousand of them are not inhabited. With 245 million inhabitants, Indonesia is the fourth-most-populous country in the world. Bali is rather small, with a population of three million. It is nicknamed the "Island of the Gods" not only because of its amazing beauty and generous nature but because of the Hindu belief that it belongs to many Gods and to the spirits of their ancestors.

By the eighteenth century, Balinese princes brought high priests from both Hindu and Buddhist religions from India. They adopted the three Hindu gods Vishnu (the guardian), Brahma (the creator), and Shiva (the destroyer). Everywhere you go there are temples. These are places of worship, and there are at least three temples in each village, one for each of these three gods. To please the gods, people craft pretty decorations from palm tree leaves and other offerings, such as flowers and fruit, to display daily. They honor the gods and believe that activities such as dancing, painting, and music make the gods happy. Bali has its own dialect, but since Indonesian independence in 1945, they also have a national language. Children learn to speak Balinese at a very young age, before they start school; in school they learn Indonesian. Everyone is bilingual.

Experiencing life outside of America would be a blessing to any American. My very first impression at the airport and in the city of Senur was of poverty. I immediately felt so appreciative of living in United States of America. I am grateful for my ancestors and the sacrifices that brought them from England to America, and for parents who raised me in Utah. I ask myself, "Why is this so? What did I do to deserve such a special circumstance, and what was I going to do to be deserving of that legacy?" I realized that responsibility comes with these blessings! I know I could choose not to appreciate what has been given, or I could move forward with a clear intention of building on this foundation and leaving a legacy for my own posterity.

My own life's experiences have led me to believe that *we* have the power and authority to create our life world, our reality. A person can choose to be happy by focusing on all the positive things in his or her life with gratitude. Embrace the moment! There are always things to learn and experience. The only thing in life that is a sure thing is change—constant change.

It serves all of us if we learn to go with the flow, to accept those things we cannot change, and to move forward with a positive perspective. I believe that's why we came to this physical existence, to *learn*, to discover ourselves, and to be creators. I believe that we came to manifest our own divinity to God. Our answers are within us, but we know that we never really arrive and there is always more to learn. We can discover the true power that is in each of us to create whatever we want, with God and our angels at our side waiting for us to ask for their assistance.

I have much gratitude for my parents who instilled in me basic value of integrity: *be your word*. If you say that you are going to do something, do it no matter what it takes. Other important values that I was taught were hard work, personal responsibility, service and compassion toward others, enthusiasm for life, and attitude. My mother always said that the three most important words in the English language are *attitude, attitude,* and *attitude*. These values have guided me through my life and are the foundation of my belief system.

CHAPTER 2

I had a wonderful childhood! I was born in Logan, Utah. I was raised in Ogden until I was five years old and then moved to Salt Lake City. I was the middle of three girls. When I was young, I was chubby, had big blue eyes, and a head full of blonde curls. I was a towhead. I was born pigeon-toed. I loved to dance, and my mother put me in ballet at a very young age to turn my feet out. I think that my feet were longer than I was tall, and by age twelve I was taller than all the boys. I was the girl that chased the boys, caught them, and held them down so that the other girls could kiss them. I became a real tomboy; I loved to do all the "guy things." I climbed trees, built forts, rode dirt bikes, and played ball yet loved playing dress-up and enjoyed my doll collection.

I also had a brother who was two years older than I, William Jr., or Billie, as we called him. He passed away when he was eighteen months old. My parents believe that it was a reaction to the DPT immunization shot. He died in my father's arms. My older sister was Melody Lynn; my little sister, Kathryn Marie. All four of us were two years apart. My mother was very busy!

Melody was the beauty queen; being beautiful always seemed to come natural to her. We called her our Cleopatra. She was gorgeous, with big, blue-green eyes, lots of thick, long eyelashes, plump rosebud lips, peaches-and-cream skin. Melody won lots of beauty pageants, and she was really into makeup and fashion. Moreover, she has been an example of courage, strength, and determination to me. She has a heart of gold.

Kathryn—we call her Kathy—was a doll. She was very thin and had beautiful dark hair and fair skin. Her bright blue eyes sparkled. Kathy was born with a hole in her heart and had one of the first open heart surgeries in Utah, back in the early sixties. She was one of the few children who survived that particular surgery. I always wanted to take care of her. Kathy is very giving and compassionate. She has always been by my side when I needed support. She is just that kind of person. We remain close to this day.

I only vaguely remember our home in Ogden, but I do remember when I was about four years old I got mad at my mother for some reason. I told her that I would just run away and that she would never see me again! She smiled and said, "Oh, are you sure? I love you, and we would miss you so much!" I was sure of it and ran to my room to pack my little doll's suitcase. As I filled the suitcase with what I thought I would need, my mother came in and said, "Please, let me help you. You probably will need a sweater," as she put one in my little doll suitcase. I was a little shocked that she was so eager to help me, but I continued to finish my packing. She hugged and kissed me good-bye and stood at the door waving to me as I left the house and walked up the street. I kept thinking, *where am I going to go? It's so scary out here in this big world!* I turned around and ran home to the loving arms of a wonderful mother who was teaching me personal choices at a very young age.

I was raised a member of the Church of Jesus Christ of Latter-day Saints. It is part of who I am today. The values and opportunities for service were fabulous! I am thankful that I had that support growing up. My mother has always been very spiritual and has been a huge positive influence for me in growing in that capacity. I remember several experiences growing up that proved to me that angels walked with me. My mother used to tell me that angels sang when I was born; she knew I had a unique purpose in life. I believe everyone has a unique purpose in life. No matter what tough things I had to go through in my youth that is one of the thoughts that carried me through. I knew if the angels sang, I was supposed to accomplish something special. I didn't know what, but it gave me confidence and made me feel special. At that age I deserved to hear that, for it assisted in building my self-esteem.

We had a cabin in Midway, Utah, where I have lots of wonderful memories of growing up. Reflecting on being protected by my angels, it was there in those beautiful mountains that I had several such experiences. You could say that I was the accident-prone one of my siblings, or that I had to learn a few hard lessons. I was always stepping on rusty nails, getting into stinging nettle, or being stepped on by horses, and I even fell out of a truck going forty-five miles an hour! To explain that last event, one of the highlights at our cabin was to load everyone up in the back of our 1957 jeep truck, called the Freedom Flyer, as the sun was going down; we would drive all over the mountains looking for deer and other wild animals. It was so exciting! My dad had a big spotlight on the top of the cab, and we would shine that all over the mountainside. It was really bright. One night we had driven into town before our deer-hunting excursion, and as we were traveling back, at a good clip on a two-lane road, I got pushed off the tool chest in the back of the truck. I remember falling and landing on the roadside. I landed on my hands and right knee, and I hit my head on the road. I looked up to see my dad driving away! I jumped up and started running after the truck, dripping in my own blood! When my father realized he had lost one of his own, he backed up and jumped out of the truck. When he got to me, I fainted in his arms! They took me home to doctor me up. I was blessed that this event wasn't any worse. I was miserable for a few days, but I survived.

We rode Tote Gotes all over those mountains. Tote Gotes were the old-fashioned mountain bike that looked like half of a modern four-wheeler. They had big thick tires and climbed those hills easily. Often, we would pack a picnic and disappear for hours up into the hills! We loved to build forts, hike, fish, and ride horses. We even had our very own horse at one time. She was a beautiful Arabian/Quarter horse with two white-stockinged feet; thus, we called her "Goodie Two Shoes." My friend, Doug would ride his horse up from the valley to meet me at a pond located just down from my cabin. We would strip the saddles and take our horses swimming. I loved that! Afterwards we would ride bareback through the fields until the horses had dried off. Those were some amazing memories we created!

One of our favorite things to do was swing over the gulley on a log attached to a rope that my father secured to a big branch of a large tree. We climbed up to the highest side of the mountain, and away we went, out over the gulley. It was like flying! Mom and Dad told us never to hold on by our hands. My father said, "Always sit on the log, and hold on tight. You wouldn't want to fall off." One day we were swinging, and I was trying to impress some cute boys who had been showing off by holding the log with their hands. I said to them, "I can do that!" So I went for it, and at the highest point my hands slipped. I fell through the trees to the bottom of the canyon, probably about sixty feet! I still remember falling. I felt no fear at all. It was as if I were just floating through the air, and when I hit the ground, I had no pain. I know now that the branches of the trees slowed my fall. I felt my angel's arms around me. I have never forgotten that feeling of love and protection.

My father was at my side quickly, took me back to the cabin, and laid me on the living room floor. My mother dressed my wounds. We were high up in the mountains, with no phone at the cabin, and cell phones did not exist. (How did we ever make it through childhood in the old days?) As I screamed in pain, my sisters ran to the player piano and began playing the song "Born Free," singing it at the top of their lungs! Their singing drowned out my screaming and took my mind off the pain. I had friction burns all over my body and a gash down my back. I recall my father saying a prayer over me, blessing me that I would sleep, and I did. I learned the value of obedience to my mother and father that day. I also realized how I was protected and that I still had a life to live. I was so high up and I fell so far that it really amazes me that I am here to tell that story.

I realize now how important our childhood experiences are. Our experiences are internalized, becoming part of who we are. Ages one through seven constitute the most important time for a child to absorb everything that is beautiful and positive in life, through all of their senses. It is important that parents and teachers are sensitive to that. I am grateful to my parents for allowing me to experience so much at such an early age. I was given the opportunity to participate in the arts, dance, music, sports, and outdoor activities. We were able to choose what we liked by experiencing it all. It also brought balance into our lives. We were taught to work hard and productively, but when it came time to play, we did that with enthusiasm.

I watched as Melody constantly challenged my mother in all kinds of ways and then learned from her experiences. We had a nice big garden that had to be weeded, so every Saturday it was our routine. My mother gave each of us a tablespoon, and we sat on the ground to dig dandelions from our lawn, one by one. It was a tedious job and something that we didn't enjoy too much, but I realize now that my mother was teaching us discipline and hard work. On this particular Saturday, Melody decided she was going on the bus into town with her girlfriend to shop instead of working with the rest of us. Melody did ask permission to go—several times, in fact—but my mother continued to say no. Melody paid no attention to that and went inside the house to get ready. About an hour later, she came out dressed in her black-and-white checkered skirt and jacket, her hair perfectly done in a flip, and her white gloves and purse in hand. In that day and age we dressed up to go downtown. She said, "Mom, I'm meeting Wendy and going downtown, okay?" My mother, without raising her voice at all said, "No, I told you we are working out here in the yard today, and you are not going downtown." Melody began to cry, having a mini tantrum, saying, "But I'm all ready to go!" My mother had the hose in her hand, watering her roses. Without saying a word, she turned around and hosed Melody from head to toe! I remember that lesson probably as much as my sister does!

I believe that the greatest discovery of all time is that a person can change their future by merely changing their mind and their attitude. In my family we were never allowed to whine or fall into a victim mode. Mom would say, "Grow up and put a smile on your face. That is life! If you think life is easy, it will be hard, but if you know it can be hard, it will be easy. Life takes courage, and when you believe in yourself, everything is possible." We would work through our emotions without imposing them on others, in our own space, usually the bedroom. I believe my mother's tough-love approach was to prepare me for the future and the experiences that I would have. I also think I was blessed with a positive gene, as I tend to look at life in a more positive light. My life has opened up many opportunities for me to share my enthusiasm for life.

I remember when I was nine or ten we lived in Salt Lake City. We had a beautiful home on the corner of Laird Avenue and Thirteenth East. We had a patch of clovers in our lawn, and I told my mother that I wasn't coming in until I found a four-leaf clover. I stayed out until after dark with a flashlight; I just knew that if I didn't give up, I would find one. Everyone thought I was just being stubborn, but guess what? I found what I was looking for! My very own, four-leaf clover. It was my first real lesson in determination. Decide what you want, have passion, and do not give up! I'll never forget the feeling of accomplishment. That has motivated me many times in my life.

When I reached twelve years of age, my awkward stage, I had low self-esteem and was learning about being a teenage girl. I was just trying to figure out growing up. I felt that I was the ugly duckling, compared to my sisters. I was chubby, awkward, with glasses and crooked teeth, I felt very insecure with my appearance. Melody and Kathy would tell me, "Don't worry, Bonnie; you have a good personality." But I wanted so badly to be pretty!

I remember asking a particular boy to the girls' choice dance after school. I was so excited that he said yes! I made a new dress, and my mother gave me a beautiful cat broach to wear on it. The day of the dance, this young man came up to me and said he had a dentist appointment but would meet me at the dance. I stood and waited through the whole dance, and he never showed. I was devastated and so embarrassed. It sure didn't do much for my self-esteem. I walked home with a broken heart and cried the whole way. When my mother consoled me, I told her I was ugly and that no boys liked me, that I would never have a boyfriend. She proceeded to teach me about visualization. She said to think of myself as beautiful: visualize it, believe it, and I would become it! Whenever I felt insecure or doubted myself, I would visualize how beautiful and smart I really was and not allow others to intimidate me. I learned to step forward, not back, to face the challenge of that feeling that comes from ego. I have used that lesson in my life over and over. I have gratitude for a wise mother who took the time to love and share with me.

CHAPTER 3

I sensed that there were problems between my parents. My father was hardly ever home, only on some weekends. My mother began to work more, to assist with providing for the family. My experiences of the specific circumstances of my parents' divorce strengthened me in many ways.

My father was a bishop in the Church of Jesus Christ of Latter-day Saints in Salt Lake City. He was excommunicated because of infidelity, and he was caught living as a polygamist. The Mormons practiced polygamy at the time Utah was settled, but when Utah became a state, the lifestyle was abolished. Many who believed in polygamy have tried to keep it alive to this day. This is one of the main reasons my mother divorced him. We did not live this principle in our home, but my father lived it in secret.

As a young girl who loved her daddy very much, I was devastated as I sat on the stairs of our home and watched him walk away, get into his car, and drive out of my life. It was traumatic for me at that time, but as I grew to understand more of the situation, I was able to release any negative feelings and look at the positive. In a civil marriage, not in his polygamy church, my father married another wonderful woman; she already had five children, and then she and my father had five more. I had acquired five step-brothers and step-sisters and five half brothers and half sisters, and each one of them has brought something wonderful into my life. My father wrote a book about his life called *Hope Heals*. My father, William Paul Hansen, passed away at the age of seventy-eight, from prostate cancer and after several years of battling Parkinson's disease, in May 2006 in St. George, Utah. I had the opportunity to have him in my home during those last days. I'm thankful for that.

After the divorce, we moved into an apartment on South Temple. My mother worked long hours to support us, doing makeovers for people out of our home and selling Shaklee's Basic "H" door to door. I went to work cleaning apartments for the tenants. I created my own little cleaning business at the age of twelve, and later I worked as a hostess at an Italian restaurant across the street, Michelino's. Eventually, I worked as a waitress. I saved enough money to pay for my college.

A few years later, my mother married Franklin W. Gunnell. They had worked together in the Utah legislature. Frank was the Speaker of the House of Representatives, and mom was his assistant and messenger. Frank was truly an inspiration to me in so many ways. He was strong, highly self-motivated, successful, and competitive. He served as a politician, Speaker of the House of Representatives for the State of Utah for seven years. He was a conservative, cherished the Constitution, and loved America. He inspired me to appreciate what our ancestors and founding fathers had done for us. He brought to my attention how blessed we are to live in America, with the ability to create our own abundance within the system of free enterprise and capitalism. The one thing that I still hear Frank saying to me is, "Don't just read history— make a little!" I have never forgotten that advice and have used that principle to push myself out of my comfort zone. Thank you, Frank, for the example you were to me.

High school was a challenge. I had a difficult time focusing; I wanted to play and just have a good time. I had a lot of bottled-up emotions about my broken family and myself. I felt a little awkward and insecure. There were lots of friends in my life and in many different cliques, and I never really fit into just one group. I tried to make friends with everyone. I got caught up in the diet/binge cycle: starving myself with Tab cola and red licorice all week, then eating pizza and ranch burgers all weekend. My weight fluctuated up and down the scale. By my junior year I weighed about 185 pounds, and I was five feet eight and a half. High school was a challenge for my grades too. I couldn't settle down and concentrate on learning. I was all about having a good time and social opportunities.

My mother was involved with an honor society program for high-school-age girls called Cotillion. I was able to participate in that program in my junior year. It intended to teach young girls etiquette, and at end of the year we were presented to society by the governor of Utah at a grand ball in the capitol rotunda. This was a big deal! The program took only a certain number of girls, and they all excelled in beauty and talent. I met girls from all over Salt Lake Valley, and we all enjoyed service projects, etiquette classes, and sharing our talents. I was motivated to be my best when I was surrounded by such amazing girls. However, with that comes the pressure of trying to be perfect, and that can present a barrier to being who you are. I had to learn to strive for progress, not perfection, and to never feel that I had to apologize for who I was. As Gerard Way said, "being happy doesn't mean that everything is perfect. It means that you've decided to look beyond the imperfections."

I am so grateful to be a woman and this offered the opportunity for me to learn grace and poise. We walked with books on our heads, squeezed quarters with our booties, and learned how to set a formal dining table and which fork to use first at dinner. We attended museums, the symphony, and the ballet and were exposed to opportunities to serve in the community. I learned to appreciate the arts as part of my upbringing. I was taught that finding your talents, developing them, and sharing them was important. I learned to play the piano, the violin, and the guitar, and of course I danced ballet. I loved ballet and took it for many years. I was to the point of dancing on toe shoes, which takes a lot of training. I really don't remember why I quit, but I will always remember my teacher, Jean Renee, who danced with Ballet West. She definitely influenced my life with the concept of discipline.

After I graduated from high school, I had to earn my own tuition and prove myself before my mother would assist me with college. I had to set some goals of what I was to accomplish. I still struggled with my weight constantly. I was in Provo, Utah, going to college, and I remember the day that I was driving down University Boulevard on my way to school when I saw a woman who was probably three hundred pounds. As I watched her struggle to even walk down the street, I knew that could be me someday if I didn't commit to changing my lifestyle. That was a huge "aha moment." I committed to making changes in my life. I got my roommates to go to the BYU track with me, and we started by walking a mile per day eventually working our way up to running five miles a day. I started to get involved with all sorts of physical activities such as; bike riding, dancing, volley ball, and flag football. These things would assist me in moving towards an active lifestyle. I also learned that it was important to surround myself with active people for support. I became interested in nutrition and I started my life journey into wellness never looking back. I took personal responsibility of creating a future of health and wellness. I am thankful for that day, when I made that conscious choice.

I loved Provo and the freedom it gave me to be on my own. I had great roommates and lots of friends. I was able to live the college life. While I was in school, I got involved as much as I could in extracurricular activities. To encourage me to be active and continue to lose weight, I even tried out for cheerleader. I had always wanted to be a cheerleader in high school but never had the confidence to try out. Now that I was starting a whole new chapter in my life I said to myself, "Why not?" So I made a conscious decision to leave my comfort zone, and the next thing I knew I was part of the cheerleading squad. What a blast we had! Of course, there are always romances between athletes and the cheerleaders, right? Well, that's what happened to me. I fell in love with one of the players on the basketball team.

After graduating and getting my degree in the medical field, I began working full-time. Dave and I had dated the whole year, so we were ready to take it a step further. Dave asked me to marry him. I was flattered, but we were still so young. Like most young couples who are in love, we liked to make out. There was a line drawn on how far we would take it. I have to admit I was the one saying no all the time! It started to cause tension in the relationship. I knew what I wanted for my future, and I didn't want to mess that up! I was raised with morals, to save myself for marriage. That is what I wanted.

One night after a basketball game, we went back to Dave's house and began to make out. Without going into too much detail, it got out of hand, and he wasn't responding to no. I had many feelings about that experience. I was traumatized, and I cried hysterically! Those emotions of pure terror and victimization were overwhelming. At the time I felt so powerless. I didn't want a fight or for him to be mad at me, and he was a big, strong guy. Afterward came the guilt, the feeling that it was my fault, and the worry that I could get pregnant. Looking back, I see it was what they now call date rape. I couldn't believe that someone who said he loved me could become that controlling and mean. I ended the relationship and realized he wasn't for me. I deserved different! Dave continued to stalk me for years after. He would appear every so often, in places I never would expect to see him, or he would call me on the phone out of the blue. Eventually the stalking stopped. He got married and had children. Years later, he took his own life, because he developed depression and became addicted to the use of drugs. I felt compassion for his family. I learned a lot in that relationship about how important it is to love and respect yourself, and I would never put myself in that situation again. We cannot put the responsibility on someone else to make us happy. It's not fair to them or you. I was so young and so in love … or I thought it was love.

This was one of my first opportunities to learn about releasing the past. My wonderful parents counseled me, "It is water under the bridge. Forgive yourself, forgive Dave, release it, and move on with your life. Don't look back with regrets! There is no need to tell anyone else about it. It's between you and God." It was a process I had to go through, but I am grateful for wise parents.

CHAPTER 4

Provo is where I met the man I chose to be my husband and father of my children "for time and all eternity." My girlfriend Judi had dated Boyd before he left on his mission for the Church of Jesus Christ of Latter Day Saints. We became roommates while he was gone. Boyd returned home after two years in the mission field, and the first time I met him was at our apartment. We became friends, as he hung out with us quite often. Judi had a boyfriend by then, so that is when Boyd and I started to date. Boyd and I dated for about six months and decided to marry.

We were married in the LDS Temple in Salt Lake City, on November 22, 1977. It was the beginning of a new chapter in my life. Our reception was held at The Homestead in Midway, Utah. That was the beginning of my thirty-year journey of learning and experiencing more than I could have ever imagined at that time. I was so young and naive! I was taught that the "purpose of life" was marriage and procreation, so that is what I felt I was to do. Marriage was an adjustment, but I think I flowed into it pretty easily. I loved being a wife and a mother. I realize now that I was in love with the idea of marriage: having a husband, children, and a family. I loved Boyd, but I didn't really know what true love was at that stage of my life. I do know now that you can love lots of different people in a lifetime, in many different ways. Boyd had a lot of great qualities and was an adventurous spirit. We certainly had a lot of fun together, and I knew he would make a great father. He was the only boy, with four sisters; I loved his family. We enjoyed a lot of lake activities. Boyd got into competitive waterskiing, and I was right there with him. He was a lot like my father, always providing activities for our family such as boating, snowmobiling, ATVs, dirt bikes, or Harley motorcycle riding. I thought our lifestyle was perfect.

After we married, we lived in a duplex in Provo our first year and then bought our first home in Orem. It was a cute little house in an older neighborhood. I worked for an oral maxillofacial clinic, with surgeons Dr. DaCosta Clark, Dr. Lowell Anderson, and Dr. Niles Herod. Maxillofacial doctors are specialists in surgery to treat many diseases, injuries and defects of the head, face, neck, jaws and the hard and soft tissues of the mouth, jaws and face region. I was their personal surgical assistant in the office and at the hospital. I received great training from some of the best doctors in Utah.

While working there I was experiencing jaw clicking, so the doctors suggested that I have treatment. This consisted of wearing braces for two years to create an overbite and then having mandibular osteotomy (jaw surgery to slide my jaw forward). I had braces when I was twelve years old, but the doctor hadn't extracted teeth, and my teeth had shifted. So here I was, twenty-five years old, with TMJ problems. TMJ is the joint that forms and contributes to the movement of the jaw. I agreed to the procedure; I knew they would take good care of me. It was the first time that I had been through surgery or in a hospital. I was always on the other side of things, being a nurse. I was really nervous. It was such a difficult experience. I didn't have any idea that it would be so miserable. After surgery my face was twice its size, my family couldn't even recognize me, and my jaw was wired shut. I could have only liquids for four months. It remains the longest four months of my life.

You would think I would lose weight, right? The first week I lost a few pounds, but then I couldn't be satisfied sipping liquids. I had lots of shakes and smoothies, and I consumed a lot of calories in trying to get the satisfaction of food. I would drink until my stomach felt it was going to pop. It was a happy day when I got my wires clipped and I opened my mouth for the first time since the surgery. I had to work it slowly. I am still slightly numb on my lower left lip because of the trauma to the mandibular nerve which runs through the lower part of the jaw. It is the nerve that the dentist numbs before he fills your lower teeth. So my lower lip on the left side always feels like I've just been to the dentist. I've learned to live with it, no big deal. I made the choice to do the procedure, so I had a good attitude and did not whine about it. I now have a beautiful smile as a result. I guess I can say it didn't come easy; I appreciate my teeth and smile even more now, and want to take care of them.

After getting that behind me, Boyd and I moved to southern Utah. Boyd managed Milne Jewelry for a year or so and then went to Southland Corporation, where he managed the 7-Eleven convenience store on St. George Boulevard, and I worked for a dentist. We moved into a small trailer—one half of a trailer, I should say—by Dixie College. It was tiny, but it was our home. We were there until we sold our home in Orem and we ended up in a home out on Lava Flow Drive, in the Santa Clara area. It was a beautiful, newly developed area. We lived there for a few months before I got a job managing a brand-new apartment complex. This was a HUD (Housing and Urban Development, government-subsidized) complex. The fifty apartments were one-, two-, and three-bedrooms. Boyd and I lived onsite, as I was provided with living accommodations, phone, and all utilities.

Managing these units was truly an eye-opener for me in many ways. I was such a trusting person and never imagined that people would not be honest with me. There was a waiting list to fill the units, and there was a mound of paperwork for each tenant. I had to call several references and verify income. Rent was based on income, and the government would subsidize each apartment accordingly. It amazed me that people would lie or try to get away with not doing their share. I would think that brand-new units would be taken care of, but nope! The constant upkeep was unreal. It was my first awareness of what entitlement benefits can do to people. I have to say not everyone takes advantage of the system, but there are plenty of them that do, and they are teaching their children to do the same. I know the system assists lots of deserving people, and it is not wrong to use this system. What I feel is wrong is people taking advantage, being complacent, and not being honest. There are so many options for people to choose from; they don't have to stay in that position. It reinforced in me the personal desire and responsibility to always work hard, smart, and honestly, no matter what I did. It's easy to fall into a victim role and blame everything on everybody else: society, economy, the spouse, our parents, or the boss. It is easy not to take responsibility for our lives and our situations. We create our own reality! Situations arise in all of our lives; what we do with them is our choice. Dealing with the people with the entitlement mentality wore me out. It forced me to grow up and see the world outside my own perception. This job served us for a few years, but I was ready to move forward, and I did.

I eventually started my own exercise program called Body Works by Bonnie. I had three classes, Monday through Friday, at a discotheque in St. George. I eventually merged with a friend, Karen Westfall, who had the Jazzerobics program. I had become pregnant with my first child and needed some assistance with the program that I had built. Together, we built the largest dance and exercise studio in southern Utah. We sponsored aerobic competitions, and I even competed in a few! A couple of years later, after my babies were born, Mark and Vicki Sorenson asked me to develop an aerobic dance and exercise program for their facility, National Institute of Fitness. It was located at the base of those beautiful red rocks in Snow Canyon, Ivins, Utah. It attracted those that wanted to make a lifestyle change and lose weight. The locals called it the "fat farm." NIF offered a great program to learn and experience the basic principles of fitness and how to live a healthy lifestyle. I was at the resort by six o'clock every morning and led participants in a stretch and then a hike up into Snow Canyon. We had lunch and were then off to various fitness classes all afternoon. I did motivational workshops and game night in the evenings. It was a wonderful time in my life. I loved what I did and developed so many awesome relationships as I inspired women and men to move more.

After five short years of marriage and, two children, choices were made, that affected my trust in my marriage. I was afraid of what might happen, because I had two baby boys. Did I want to raise them alone? Did I want to be a single parent? I had made a commitment to marriage. Could I hold to the idea of eternal marriage? I felt so many emotions and had so many fears of the future.

As a wife and a mother, I wanted to do everything I could to keep my family together. My little boys, Tyler, age two, and Trevor, three months, gave me the strength and courage to do what I needed to do. I was determined not to be a single mother, so that

I could provide a stable home for them. Like all relationships, ours had ups and downs. It certainly wasn't all bad; we created some wonderful memories. I worked hard at serving God, my family, church, community, and work. To fill the void in my relationship with my husband, I stayed very busy and filled my life with other positive things and people. Boyd and I were really into raising our sons, and they went everywhere with us. In all our years of marriage, we took only two trips without them. It was so much fun to have our boys with us. We bought a condominium on Beaver Mountain, Utah, and it was our little getaway. We created lots of memories on that mountain!

Section 2

Live the Present

CHAPTER 5

Children are the bridge to heaven.
                                    —Persian proverb

In Bali newborn babies are very sacred, because they have just
come from the gods. For the first year of their lives they are
carried; their feet are never allowed to touch the ground, which is
considered to be impure. The new baby is considered too fragile to
touch the ground where the evil spirits are. There is a ceremony in
which the priest places the child's feet on the ground for the very
first time, on the first birthday, or a complete Balinese cycle of 210
days. After the ceremony the child is symbolically freed from the
mother's womb and now belongs to the human world—a place
more remote from the gods but closer to the family.

Another custom in Bali is giving a child's first name in accordance
of birth order. There are four groups, and they can be used for
either a girl or a boy. When the first child is born, whether a girl
or a boy, its name must be Wayan or Puta or, only if it is a boy,
Gedi. The secondborn, girl or boy, is called Made or Kadek; the
thirdborn is Nyoman or Komang; and the fourth one, Ketut.
After the fourth child, one starts all over again. It can get quite
challenging if you have more than four children! To make it a
little easier to know if the name belongs to a boy or a girl when

reading the name, one writes "NI" before a girl's name and "I" before a boy's name.

In each family, there is no common last name. There are no family names passed down from generation to generation. The parents decide on the last name individually. They wait about three months for the chance to get to know the characteristics of the child. Some children get names based on the way they look; others are named according to their personality traits.

I think about how Boyd and I were blessed with our three beautiful boys, and each one had his own unique personality. Tyler John (June 6, 1981) and Trevor Chase (June 10, 1983) were born in St. George, Utah, and Trenton Boyd (November 28, 1989) was born in Newton, New Jersey.

Tyler was challenging for me right from his birth. I flowed through pregnancy with him, but my water broke early, and I had an emergency C-section. Looking back, it was a little overwhelming. How thankful I was for the medical team that delivered him to us! As a new baby, he was always fussing. I know now that a big part of that was because I, as a new mother, was a little nervous and overprotective. My sister, Kathy, always laughed about me taking a flashlight in Tyler's room at night to check on him. Tyler was my firstborn, and that made him special in my eyes. He was strong-willed, and we knew that from the very beginning. He kept to himself, quiet and reserved but he was a very hard worker. He enjoyed projects and working alongside his dad. He loved motor sports; dirt biking, snowmobiling, and ATV's. Tyler was dedicated to achieving his Eagle Scout award; when he received it, he was so excited! Team sports weren't his thing. He gravitated to independent sports and was very good at everything he tried. As Tyler grew and matured, I saw the great person he was. He was a wonderful son.

Trevor was so much easier for me. Of course, I had experience by then. I had a scheduled C-section this time and was awake as I delivered. It was tough, but my little boy shocked us all, because we thought he would be a girl! This pregnancy had been so different than my first, and the ultrasound couldn't tell us one way or the other. He was born with a happy disposition. Everyone loved him, and other kids gravitated to him. He had such a big smile and a big heart! He was very sensitive, compassionate, and giving. When the ice cream man came to our neighborhood, Trevor would buy ice cream with his own allowance for those friends who did not have any money. He loved life and lived every moment to the fullest. He was athletic like Tyler but loved team sports. He was the star of every team that he played on. A natural athlete!

Tyler and Trevor were best friends and did everything together. It was almost like having twins, they were so close. They did have their times of conflict, as do most siblings, but overall they enjoyed each other very much.

Trenton was delivered six years later via a scheduled C-section. I had general anesthesia, so the recovery was more difficult. He was my surprise package and, I knew, a real blessing from God. He was such a good baby, and the other boys loved helping me with him. Trevor particularly watched over Trenton, holding him as a baby, rocking him to sleep, taking hold of his little hand if needed. He would run to his side if he made the slightest peep. I was able to enjoy the baby stage with Trent, as I was much more relaxed as a mother. As Trent got older, the boys liked to tease him, so there was a lot of interaction and noise. As Trent grew up I could see a perfect blend of qualities in his little personality that resembled both of his brothers in some ways, but his own unique self shone. He has insight into living life that a lot of people never get in a whole lifetime. He is loving, compassionate, respectful, and a lot of fun. Trent is an example of thoughtfulness and service everywhere he goes.

What an honor to be the mother of three amazing sons. I am truly blessed!

CHAPTER 6

My sister, Melody, lived in Sparta, New Jersey, with her family. In 1984 she found Boyd an employment opportunity with D&R Boats in Dover, New Jersey. We decided to take this job and have the experience of living outside of Utah. Tyler and Trevor were young and not in school yet, so we thought it was perfect timing. Living on the East Coast was great! I met wonderful people of all kinds. It was my first experience living outside of Utah. We lived there six years.

We struggled financially, and there were times I really don't know how we fed our family. Boyd was in and out of several jobs, doing the best he could to provide. I worked at Vernon Valley Great Gorge Spa, teaching fitness classes, and began working with Melody at the company she developed, the first total appearance, personal development, and image corporation. I was an image consultant in the afternoon while my children were taking their naps. I marketed our holistically formulated products, skincare, makeup, and nutritional supplements from my dining room table. I could be home while raising a family and have a flexible and exciting career. I also traveled with Melody to present workshops to corporations in New York City, and we worked with national and state beauty pageants.

Melody's image consulting company focused on nutrition, fitness, personality profile, dressing for success, color analysis, skincare, makeup, and figure analysis. The personality profile was put together specifically for her company by the dean of psychology at Fairleigh Dickinson University. The profile has four categories: competitive, enthusiastic, sociable, and precise. We all have these personality traits in us, but to different degrees. The profile was the foundation of our consultations.

Competitive people are born leaders. They thrive on challenges and risks and are creative and self-motivated. The competitive personalities generally have their own businesses or CEO and management positions.

Enthusiasts are motivators and love the limelight. They can excite others with whatever they are excited about. They are great with people and are drawn to the sales and marketing field or other careers that offer the opportunity to motivate others.

The sociable individual is conservative. These folks get along with all personalities, because they are not a threat. The most compassionate of all the personalities, they tend to take things more personally and are very sensitive to how others treat them. Their organizational skills give them the ability to recognize the need for improvement or change.

Precise individuals are very detailed in everything they do. They are analytical and tend to be employed in the fields of computing, accounting, etc. These individuals are loyal and trustworthy. They want to know exactly what is expected of them. It is important for them to have a daily schedule at work and at home

Dressing for success and the psychological effect of color was a popular concept in the eighties, and I believe it holds true today. I realized that it does make a difference in how others respond to you. Telling the right story about yourself in this way can make a big difference. Society is very visual, and you can learn to use that to your advantage. When competing in the job market, Melody's motto was "Dress for the job you want, not the job you have."

I particularly became very interested in the different personalities and realized how it helped me understand people and the relationships in my own life. I enjoyed doing workshops for the youth, being a positive influence and teaching them how important it is to project who they really are, to respect and honor themselves in the way they act and look in such a way that others will see it too.

You can be the most spiritual, moral, honest, healthy, motivated, great person in the whole world, but if you look the opposite of that, you will attract the opposite sort of people. That includes how you carry yourself, knowing you are the best that you can be. You have self respect and self love. If you want others to want to get to know you this way, dress and carry yourself to project that which you want to attract. You are telling a story about yourself.

CHAPTER 7

Even animals have their own unique personalities, and Bali was full of wild animals that roam free on the island. There are many monkeys there, and we stayed right outside the "Monkey Forest" in Ubud. They just love to take anything right out of a person's hands if they can! The babies are so cute. They hang on and ride underneath their mother's tummy. The only remaining elephants in Bali were imported from Sumatra. At the Bali Safari and Marine Park, I was able to ride an elephant named Kuta, which means "happy-go-lucky," escorted by his trainer Wayan. It was fun riding through the jungle on the back of the elephant. We saw zebras, white tigers, monkeys, rhinos, and all sorts of beautiful birds. It was also exciting that we were able go to Komodo Island to see the Komodo dragons. These dragons can be seen only in Indonesia and are becoming extinct. They prey on their own babies. A Komodo dragon looks like a huge crocodile, with short legs, a long scaly body, and a tongue that goes in and out like a snakes. Their mouths secrete toxins, and the venom paralyzes their victims. They move slowly but are very powerful.

Most Balinese families have a dog, because they are excellent guards. There are lots of stray dogs that look sickly and are losing their hair. I love animals, and it was so sad to see! I have always had a dog, and each one of my dogs was so special to me. Each one of them had his or her own personality too.

I was at the stage of my life where I felt I had a constantly full schedule. I was running in many directions, as mothers do with the needs of family, community, and church. But no family is complete unless they have a pet of some sort! They add so much to a family. We went to the pet store with the intention of purchasing a small dog and bought the cutest little cocker spaniel puppy. He was adorable, with big eyes full of love and cute floppy ears, and when we bought him they told us that he wouldn't get very big. He was just a small or medium-size dog. The whole family fell in love at first sight. We named him Toby. He continued to grow and grow and grow. He became the biggest cocker spaniel I had ever seen. He was just a big puppy with that much more love to give.

We lived on Lake Mohawk in New Jersey; our sloping lawn led down to our dock. Waterskiing and fishing were our favorite activities. One morning Tyler, Trevor, and Justin, their cousin, were dragging their fishing poles down the back lawn with the flies moving through the grass. Toby pounced on one and got it hooked into his jowl. Toby started yipping, and all three boys started to scream and cry. Toby yelped and the boys cried all the way to the vet. This kicked off a string of events with Toby that seemed to be never ending.

A couple of months later, Toby was chasing the car and barking as I drove up the driveway to take my sons to ball practice. I stopped, opened my door, and with authority, told him *"No! Stay!"* As I proceeded up the driveway, we immediately heard that familiar yelping sound. Oh, no! I had run over Toby! The boys began to cry and scream. I felt so bad. I wanted to cry and scream too. I had broken Toby's leg. I hustled everyone to the vet ... again. They had to put a steel pin into his leg. Poor Toby!

I had lived in Utah my whole life and grew up with dogs in our house. It never occurred to me that dogs get fleas. My dogs had never had that problem; I guess it was too dry in Utah. I'd heard of fleas but had never seen one. Well, guess what? Toby got infested with fleas. Boyd would walk down the hall, and they would jump up and cling to the hair of his legs. They were everywhere! Even in our car. We took the dog to be "dipped," and we had to fumigate our home for two weeks. During this time we flew home to Utah, since it was time for a trip home anyway.

When we returned to New Jersey after our vacation, we moved off the lake to another home that had a beautiful backyard with a forest and a river all around us. We had deer, rabbits, porcupines, and raccoons continually in our yard. Because Toby had gotten so big and destroyed things in the house, we decided to make him an outdoor dog. We built a nice doghouse with a light in it. That kept him warm. He was attached to a big chain that ran the length of the yard. He loved the freedom that the outdoors gave him. The kids spent most their time out there with Toby. He loved the boys. He would chase the animals, running the length of the chain. He became very strong and kept the wild animals in their place.

One day I came home to the sound of Toby barking out of control. When I walked around back, I saw why. He had a raccoon cornered on the porch! I knew it had to be rabid; raccoons are nocturnal and are out in the day only if they are sick. I called animal control, and they came and had us quarantine Toby for two weeks in case he had been exposed to rabies. We were glad we had Toby to protect us and keep that raccoon cornered so that animal control could take it away.

The day came that we had to move back to Utah, and we could not take Toby with us. We put an ad in the paper to see if we could find a good home for him on our own and give him to a deserving family. We thought that we had found the perfect home for him, and they came and took him for the weekend to see if everyone would get along. I told them that he was an outdoor dog, but they wanted to have him indoors with the family. I guess they were eating pizza on the bed while watching TV, when Toby jumped up to get some. The woman put her hand out, and Toby bit her! He was always so gentle with the children and had never bitten anyone. We were so surprised! They returned him that night and reported it to the authorities. We had to quarantine Toby again, this time for six weeks! What to do with that sweet puppy? We had our own *Marley and Me* stories to tell now. I'll never forget our experiences with Toby. He brought wonderful experiences into all of our lives. What a personality!

CHAPTER 8

I pretty much raised the boys alone, because Boyd commuted to the city. He left early in the morning and came home most days after dark, when the children were in bed. He worked hard to provide a living during the week and served in the bishopric for the church on the weekends. It was quite the era in my life. I loved and still love being a mother, but it was definitely a lot of work. The best advice that I received from my mother was, "The easy thing now will be the hard thing when they are older. The hard thing now will pay off to be the easy thing later!"

When my older boys were about three and five years old, my mother was visiting us in New Jersey. She was watching the frustration I had getting my boys to respond to my directions. She sat all of us down on the couch. She pointed her finger at Trevor and said, "Repeat after me: 'My mother is the boss.'" Trevor lifted his big blue eyes timidly and repeated it. Then she moved to Tyler and said, "Repeat after me: 'My mother is the boss.'" Tyler repeated the phrase. Then she looked right at me boldly and, pointing her finger in my face, said, "Repeat after me: 'I am the boss.'" She made me realize how important it was to be the boss and take the time and energy when they were young to follow through and to be consistent with my actions of discipline. It definitely can be a job!

Teaching my boys good values was a high priority for me. I had to remind myself of that quite often. My days were full. I would take one to one baseball field, drive the other one to another baseball field, run home to nurse and change my baby, then run back to the baseball fields to pick up the older boys. It went on and on and on!

Riding in the car was an event in itself. My two older boys, ages three and five, would be in the backseat fighting. One would tease the other, the other would scream and tease back, and then they would both be screaming. Ugh! I would turn around and say several times, "Please quit fighting. Mommy is driving, and it is hard to drive with you screaming!" Do you think that worked? Nope! Consistency and follow-through are very important. Never say you are going to do something and then not follow through, if you want your kids to trust and listen to you. Make sure that the consequence is something you can and will deliver. Out of frustration, I finally turned around and said, "If you don't quit fighting right now, I am pulling over, and you both can get out and walk home!" Oh, no! What had I done? We were about four blocks from home, and all these thoughts came rushing into my head: *How can I leave my little boys out here? What if they get taken? They are going to hate me. What if they get lost?* My stomach was churning with nervousness, and I almost felt lightheaded. I knew I had to follow through, so I pulled over and asked them to get out of the car. They both started crying and wouldn't budge. I got out, walked around, opened the door, and escorted them out onto the sidewalk. They were screaming! I projected calm. I didn't yell, and I was as firm and tough-loving as I could be. My heart pounding, I got back into the car and drove off. It was a hard thing to do! I went around the block, and as I pulled up behind them, I could see them both, and they were holding hands as

41

they walked toward home. I pulled over and invited them back into the car and asked, "Now when your mommy asks you to do something, will you mind her?" They both nodded their cute little heads and got in. It was quiet the rest of the trip home, and in the future if they started fighting in the car, all I had to say was, "Please stop. Do you want mommy to pull over?" That's all it took for them to quiet down. They knew their mother was true to her word.

As a mother, I'm thinking of another teaching moment that stands out in my mind. At the ages of six and eight, Tyler and Trevor came to me wanting the latest in athletic shoes: Michael Jordan shoes that lit up when you walked. Of course, all their friends had them, and it was something that they both really wanted. Those shoes were around $125! Never had I spent that much money on a pair of shoes, not even for myself. I didn't have the extra money at that time anyway. I looked at this as an opportunity to teach them the value of money, so I made a deal with them. I told them that I would pay the amount that I could afford, and they would have to pay the difference, which was thirty-five dollars. With my help the boys got creative with how they could earn the money. Those boys went to friends and neighbors to assist them with weeding, taking out garbage cans, mowing lawns, and even selling avocado hand and body lotion! After earning the money, Tyler and Trevor were pretty excited to go and buy their new shoes. The fun thing for me was watching them empower themselves to know that they could be creative in how to raise money, work hard, and be successful. I watched the way that they took care of their shoes, wiping them clean and carefully placing them in their closet. I remember them sitting in a circle with their friends, with their feet in the center, admiring the shoes as they lit up. I knew it had been worth the time to teach my boys that lesson.

My boys went everywhere with me. I even took them with me to work. While I was teaching my fitness classes they would play in the nursery and as they got older they began to help babysit the other children. After their morning at the nursery, we would stop for lunch at Subway for a kid's meal. Believe it or not, one of their favorite outings was going to the mall with me. They were so much fun! I was raised with sisters, so boys were a whole new experience for me. I have loved every single minute of being a mother of three sons. My boys were awesome!

I realized that with all the demands of life coming at a mother from all directions, it is so important to take care of yourself first, mind, body, and spirit! It takes creative solutions, but with clear intentions and openness to all possibilities, a woman can create her own time. Time for oneself! Thank goodness I had my exercise classes. Physical fitness saved me in times of difficulty and stress. I would just kick a little higher, punch a little harder, and run a little faster to stimulate those natural happy hormones that exercise produces. I was told to liken it to an airplane flight, when they tell you to put the oxygen mask on yourself first. You are not going to assist anyone if you are not balanced and healthy. If you feel good, you are able to forget yourself and take time and energy to serve others. My life has been dedicated to inspiring and teaching women that principle. It's made an incredible difference in my life.

My mother has been such a huge mentor and teacher for me, not only through example, but in the time spent in conversations. I honor the woman she is. She has been one of my greatest teachers. I know that she prepared me for the challenges I was about to experience in my adult life. As I grew into adulthood, she continually encouraged personal responsibility. I never could fall into the poor-me syndrome or the victim mode. She would tell me, "Put a smile on your face, and have a good attitude, knowing that it is just life!" Little did I know that with that philosophy, she was preparing me for the most impactful experience of my entire life. It was something that I could not control, something that in a million years I would not sign up for. It was an experience that would change my life, in more ways than one, forever.

CHAPTER 9

The roads in Bali are full of motorcycles going and coming in all directions. There were entire families on one bike, and it looked like they were just hanging on! When the women are wearing their ceremonial dresses, they ride sidesaddle, and sometimes they can be seen carrying very tall offerings. When it rains you can see some passengers holding umbrellas high above the driver. There are cars and trucks too, but most families can't afford a vehicle, which means there are far fewer of them, and more motorcycles. The most popular is a scooter called a *bebek* (the word for "duck" in Indonesian), because of its shape.

Oh, how I reflect on our many trips to our condo on Beaver Mountain in Utah. This was one of our favorite places to hike, fish, and ride dirt bikes and four-wheelers, all over the Rocky Mountains. My boys started riding holding onto my back when they were young; it wasn't long before I was holding on to the back of them! We enjoyed outdoor activities as a family. My boys learned how to work hard, but they loved to play hard too! We had motorcycles, four-wheelers, snowmobiles, snowboards, snow skis, jet skis, and everything that goes with them! Boyd and I spent as much time as we could with our boys. Being together as a family was important to me. I tried to keep a balance in my life with my family, friends, and work.

Boyd and I had always enjoyed boating and waterskiing together. We had a boat, and his uncle Don had a houseboat on Lake Powell. We spent every chance we could on the water. Boyd loved to compete, and we traveled around the state to different competitions. After we had our boys, we continued to do water sports. We lived on a lake in New Jersey and had a boat dock out our back door. Our boys started to knee-board and water ski at the young ages of three and five. I still can see Trevor behind the boat on a knee-board, holding on tight. Everyone on the lake pointed at him, and they were amazed that he was only three years old. He was fearless! I think about the courage we have when we come into this world.

In June 1991 we moved back to Utah to assist Boyd's mother, because his father was very ill. We never returned to the East Coast. His father passed away in August, and Boyd went out to New Jersey and moved all of our belongings while I enrolled the kids in school. We lived with his mother for the following year. Boyd worked in sales for a Ford dealership, then became manager of Power Sports Authority, and then moved on to Harley-Davidson as a manager. During those years at Harley, I could feel more at ease about our income and keeping up with our bills. The boys were older now, so I was working full-time and was finally able to put a little money into savings. I was still struggling in my marriage relationship with feelings that continually surfaced from past experiences. I justified staying with Boyd because there were no drugs, alcohol, or physical abuse. I would continue to fill my life with my family, my children, my friends, and my work, and it would all play out when the time was right.

After the move back to St. George, Utah, we continued to enjoy the water. We had many great times on Uncle Don's houseboat on Lake Powell. The boys continued to water ski and were quite good at it. It was amazing to watch them enjoying the sport at such a young age.

I began working for Green Valley Spa and Resort and loved it. Wellness was my niche, and Green Valley provided an amazing place to do what I loved. It was one of the leading spas to teach the balance of mind, body, and spirit. I was the fitness director, a nutrition counselor, and a personal trainer. I had the opportunity to train such celebrities as Robert Redford, Sonia Braga, Christopher Noth, Linda Evangelista, Caroline Rhea, Stockard Channing, James Gandolfini, Paula Zahn, and many more.

A highlight of my work experience at Green Valley Resort was my unique experience with Robert Redford and his girlfriend Billie. He arrived after the Sundance Film Festival for some R&R. The owner of the spa came to me and said that we had a high-profile personality coming, gave me Bob's assistant's phone number to call, and told me to keep it quiet. I called and was given his private cell phone number. I got his voice mail, so I left my name, number, and the reason for calling. It wasn't long after that I received a return message from him. He said, "Hello, Bonnie. This is Bob, Bob Redford from Sundance. I received your call and would appreciate a return call to set up personal trainings for Billie and I for when we are at Green Valley Spa. Thank you very much." I saved that message for as long as my phone would let me! I had fun having my family and friends listen. I would say, "Listen to who called me today!" When they heard his voice, it was interesting to see their response. Most of them didn't think that it was really him, but those that were Robert Redford fans were so excited.

I met Bob and Billie at their room to set up appointment times. We decided to do a variety of activities. We started with a hike behind the resort. As we hiked and looked out over the beautiful red rock terrain, it was so much fun to hear about the experiences that he had while he was filming *Butch Cassidy and the Sundance Kid*. He told me they rode horses on the same trail that Butch and Sundance did. He said he hadn't seen the movie since the premiere, until a few years ago with his grandson. He laughed and said, "It was pretty entertaining." He filmed not only that movie in southern Utah, but several others.

Throughout the week I met with them for weight training, Pilates, and yoga. Bob was a gentleman and such an inspiration. At seventy, he was so active: skiing, riding horses, and fishing. They wrote me a very nice thank-you note and gifted me with a beautiful wool blanket from Sundance Resort. They invited me to their home in northern Utah in the Provo Canyon, where he owned the resort. Maybe sometime in the future, our paths will meet again. If not, I enjoyed being with the two of them and sharing their love and enthusiasm for life.

All kinds of wonderful people came from all over the world, and I loved them. I made great friends, and I made good money. It was a flexible job to have while raising a family. It became my home away from home, and the owners of the spa, the Coombs family, became like family to me. I was there for over twenty years.

I looked for every opportunity to serve my church and community. Because of my experience with wellness, I was often asked to conduct workshops for women's events and activities. My experience in New Jersey working with Melody as an image consultant at MJIC really added to my insight into personal development for people, particularly women.

CHAPTER 10

The summer of 1996 was very eventful. My stepfather, Franklin W. Gunnell, had been ill throughout the springtime, and he just couldn't get over flulike symptoms. When he was taken into the hospital, they found that he was in the last stages of bladder cancer. He passed away in June. I spent the last week of his life with him and my mother on the ranch. Franklin and Mom had been married twenty-five years and were quite a team. They loved each other very much. He was a great man!

In August 1996, my family and I returned to Logan for the county fair before the boys went back to school. I remember thinking how great it was to be together as a family and how thankful that I was to be the mother of three awesome boys. We decided to ride our ATVs over Beaver Mountain and end up at Bear Lake, where our friends Guy and Dominee had a condo. They had invited us for a barbecue. We were all hot and dirty, so when they suggested we go out on the lake in the boat before dinner, we all agreed.

Trevor wanted to wakeboard; he went into the water, and up he came on the wakeboard. The boys always wore life jackets, and we had raised them in the water, so I never worried about them. But something went wrong that afternoon. After wakeboarding for a few minutes, Trevor suddenly let go of the rope and fell into the water.

When we circled the boat around, Trevor was floating face-down. I will never forget the panic that swept through my body! Boyd jumped into the water and tried to lift him up, with all of us trying to assist him, to no avail. Tyler, who was only fifteen years old at the time, managed to pull his brother up onto the boat all by himself. I started to administer mouth-to-mouth as we sped back to the dock. When we got him on the dock, I could not get a pulse, so I began CPR. Another man joined me and assisted. We got a pulse, and I continued to do mouth-to-mouth until the ambulance arrived. It seemed like an eternity! I stood up and my knees were bloody from kneeling on the dock. I didn't even feel them hurting at the time.

Trevor was airlifted to the Primary Children's Hospital in Salt Lake City. We got in the car and headed there. When we arrived Trevor was on life support. Trevor never regained consciousness, and twenty-four hours later we had to make the heart-wrenching decision to take him off life support.

I had kept a diary since girlhood. Throughout the years I had kept a journal and enjoyed reflecting. We think we will remember events in our lives, that these events will stay with us forever, I have learned it isn't the case. The details disappear quickly, and those memories seem to be gone forever. So when I lost Trevor I knew that journaling was important, not only to assist me in remembering, but for healing. By writing my thoughts, feelings, and emotions, I could begin to process the experience. To this day I often return to my journals, I am surprised at the things that I have forgotten and continue to discover about myself in those pages.

Journal excerpt: Monday, August 11, 1996

I'll never forget Kathy's [my sister's] look on her face as she told me, "We're losing him, Bonnie."

50

Three of the doctors sat down with Boyd and I
to tell us his brain had been deprived of oxygen
too long and he had massive swelling. We had to
take him off life support and put it God's hands.
I'll never forget the pain that ripped through my
heart. It was too unbelievable! My sweet Trevor,
I ached all over! Boyd and I were in shock. We
decided to keep him on life support until we
could gather family. I can't even name all the
family that supported us through this. Tyler and
Trent were able to see their brother and say good-
bye. After watching Frank take his last breath
a few weeks earlier, I could not watch my little
boy take his. I was so emotional, I just couldn't! I
think everyone thought that I should be in there,
but I just couldn't do it! I was so, so, so, so sad! I
Boyd and I were living a parent's worst nightmare.
We were all exhausted emotionally and physically.

Journal excerpt: Monday, August 12, 1996

Trevor passed peacefully about 1:00 a.m. Tonight
Boyd, I, and the boys stayed at mom's house in
the basement. Boyd and I had knelt in prayer and
then got into bed. I turned the light switch off of
the lamp, next to my bedside. Boyd had his head
in his pillow saying his prayer and I think he fell
asleep. I said mine and rolled over facing the lamp.
I was emotional, my heart was broken and I was
talking to Trevor, telling him how proud I was to
be his mother and that I loved him so much. Just
at that moment the lamp blinked on and off, not
just once but a couple of times! I checked the lamp

switch and the bulb to see if something was wrong
but found nothing. It was working perfectly! I just
know that it was my Trevor saying, "I love you
too, Mom, and I am OK."

Trevor's death was devastating. I had never felt that kind of pain. It
was truly the depths of sorrow. Trevor had been the peacemaker of
our family, compassionate and sensitive. He was a happy thirteen-
year-old boy, living life with vigor. My heart was broken.

Emotions flood into your reality in a time like that. Everything
seemed as if I were in a bad dream, moving in slow motion.
Family and friends rallied around us in this time of sorrow. I felt
my angel's arms around me, comforting me. I learned so much
about compassion, as I realized people shared things with us that
gave them comfort. Gratitude for the wonderful people in my life!

After the burial services, it was very difficult to leave my son at the
cemetery. I could not believe I had lost my thirteen-year-old son,
Trevor Chase. With him went a piece of my heart. I was overcome
with grief for my loss! My mother wept with me and said, "Now is
the time you focus on what you do have, not what you don't." We
wept again. It was a hurt that I could never describe, no matter
how I would try. It was a personal experience, my experience to
learn from and to grow stronger from. I knew that!

Journal excerpt: Sunday, August 16, 1996

This has been such a spiritual experience and I
am trying so hard to be strong and look for the
positive and the blessings that can come out of
this. Life must go on and my heart is so broken,
will the pain of this grief ever go away? I know

that even this experience could have been worse.
Trevor died in peace and doing what he loved!
We were together as a family and I know we did
what we could. I keep saying that God must have
needed him more than I did; he's on a mission.
We will be together again someday.

CHAPTER 11

Life goes on, but it is difficult when everyone goes on with their lives and you are left alone. You are left to hold your head high as you seek to fill the void in your life. I found that people learn to cope and survive their losses differently. The key to surviving that loss for me was to find the opportunity to serve others. Serving others and sharing my talents led me to forget about my worries. So many people choose to turn to alcohol, drugs, etc. to dull their pain; I chose to pursue healthy habits. I had been taught and had experienced mind, body, and spirit, and I knew that it would see me through this difficult time.

I was so grateful for my work! I went right back to Green Valley, teaching classes and nutrition counseling. I was so thankful for a place to go and forget myself, a place to serve and assist others with their lives. And in my time of grief, people came into my life to assist me.

Mother's Day 1997, I was doing a nutrition consultation. The woman that was sitting in my office poured her heart out to me about the trials in her life. I listened intently. All of a sudden she stopped, looked at me, and asked, "Did you lose a son recently?" I told her my story of losing Trevor the previous August. She told me that she had a gift of feeling and sensing spirit beings. She said that Trevor was present and that he wanted me to know that he was happy and joyful! That he loved me and was proud of me and the way I handled his passing, and because of that, it allowed him to move on. I broke down and wept. How could this woman, whom I never met before and haven't seen since, know these things? She described his physical characteristics precisely. I knew she was telling me the truth. My heart said so. I do believe that people have special gifts like hers, and that nothing just happens. I do believe that there is life after death and that I will see Trevor again. This experience confirmed to me what I know in my heart to be true. That day we comforted each other with our individual challenges. I will never forget it!

After Trevor's death, our family grew closer as we had more appreciation for one another. Every moment together became more precious. Tyler's personality blossomed. Everything he did seemed to be Trevor-motivated. Things that Trevor wanted to do, Tyler did. Trevor always wanted a jeep, so when Tyler got his license he bought one. Trevor wanted a landscaping business, so Tyler started a little landscaping business. I remember Tyler working hard to get his Eagle Scout award. For his big project, he built a park bench in the Bloomington Hills Park with a tribute to Trevor. He had the assistance of other scouts that were friends. I know how proud Tyler was to receive that award. It was quite an accomplishment. It was interesting to watch Tyler grow so much from that experience in his young life. It was almost as if Trevor stepped aside to allow Tyler to progress. Tyler had been always in the shadow of Trevor. Their personalities were so different, and after Trevor passed I saw Tyler begin to mature and become much more confident. Yet I know that it was devastating for Tyler when we lost Trevor; they were so close. It was devastating for all of us. What a void our Trevor left behind!

Trenton was almost seven years old when Trevor passed away. I don't know if he really grasped what was happening. I know that he missed Trevor. Just before that time, we learned that Trenton was having petit mal seizures. I didn't know what they were. We called them dazes when he went into a blank stare. Petit mal seizures are also known as absence seizures. They take the form of a staring spell: the person suddenly seems to be "absent." It really worried me when they would happen, and I didn't know how to handle it. I began to do my own research into naturopathic and homeopathic treatments. I read everything I could about it and consulted with nutritionists. I put Trenton on a strict diet, eliminating any processed foods, sugar, preservatives, yeast, or gluten, and we fed him organic food when possible. I kept a ledger of the times he had seizures: what he ate, the time, and what activity he was doing. I was looking for some kind of pattern. The seizures did not get worse, but they were still haunting us. Trenton would have anywhere between three to six seizures a day. We tried the preventative route for a year, which really built his immune system. We were referred to a homeopathic doctor in Las Vegas. They found through blood tests that he was allergic to pesticides. His immune system just couldn't handle chemicals. I went through my house and eliminated all chemicals. I began to incorporate essential oils more frequently into our lifestyle. Trenton was healthy in every other way, but those seizures would not go away. Seizures are tough because they create a pathway in the brain that has to be broken for them to stop.

So we took him to a neurosurgeon in northern Utah who told us that to make our lives a little easier, we should just put him on medication. I had tried to do what I thought was my best for my son, but I realized that there needed to be an intervention to free him from this. After about three years of personal research and effort, we finally had to put him on Depakote, a chemical brain-balancing drug that would change the pathway or pattern set in his brain. The protocol was that he would be on it for two years. Along with the medication, we continued providing him with good nutrition and kept him away from chemicals. It worked and within two weeks his seizures stopped. The wonderful thing was that after one year he was free to go off the medication, and we continued to build his health through good nutritional habits. We put him on herbs and supplements to cleanse his system and rebuild his little body. I'm so glad that I took the time and put in the extra effort of incorporating natural remedies! We found the source, eliminated it, and allowed his body to repair itself. I am also grateful for the drug that played a role in his overcoming the seizures that he was having. I feel it was a balanced treatment that worked for my son. It was a balance between modern medical treatment and naturopathic medicine. Trenton knew that he had been given a new opportunity for perfect health, and to this day he makes good choices for good health. He appreciates what he has been blessed with. I forgot what a stress that was in my life; constantly worrying about Trent. I could finally sleep at night. Moving forward, magnified by the loss of Trevor, I feared losing Trent because of his health, yet he really has been my healthiest child. We do not know what's in the plan of our lives. We move forward, doing what we have to do, learning as we go.

I had held strength for others at the expense of myself and knew I held in a lot of emotion. I started having physical symptoms. I have personal experience of how we create sickness in our bodies through harboring emotions and feelings. My left hip was affected, and I could not walk without dragging my left leg. It is to this day one of the most painful physical experiences that I have had! The hips represent balance in life, and accepting all experiences for growth and learning. It made sense to me, since I had just lost my son. It was a very difficult experience to accept. All emotion comes from either love or fear; fear is the energy that contracts, and love is the energy that forever expands. This is when I discovered Louise Hay, a metaphysical teacher. Her book *Heal Your Body* was such a blessing. As Louise Hay brings out in her book, all disease comes from fear or anger. I realized how powerful our thoughts and feelings are and how they directly affect our physical health. In my opinion, the most important emotion to recognize is forgiveness of ourselves first and then of others. When you forgive completely, you will be healthier, happier and have peace. So, I began practicing a belief system: do positive affirmations every day, as many times as I could. It changed my life! Replacing all those old thought patterns with new, wonderful and stimulating thoughts has been a big part of my healing, mentally, spiritually, and physically. I have overcome many physical symptoms in my own life, such as migraine headaches, allergies, digestive problems, anxieties, and foot, hip, and back pain. Meditation and positive affirmations have become a regular part of my day.

CHAPTER 12

I can't think of any sorrow in the world that a hot
bath wouldn't help, just a little bit.
                                            —Susan Glasee

As you move around the island of Bali, you will often notice
groups of the villagers bathing in the rivers. Traditionally, that
was their bathtub, and a joyful place to meet for the whole village.
Women are considered less pure and bathe downstream of the
men and the children all bathe together also. Today, most Balinese
have running water, but collective bathing still remains a pleasure.
It was nature that first provided showers and baths. People have
bathed in lakes, rivers, oceans, and waterfalls for centuries, and
there are still some cultures that use these gifts of nature for
cleansing.

Every evening I have a warm, relaxing bath, meditate, recite my
goals and affirmations, and express gratitude for a healthy, strong
body. It is a highlight of my day. A bath offers the therapeutic
effect of water, which relaxes the body and can take the mind
to a calm place. The opportunity to relax and reflect in a warm
bath at the end of the day has worked for me in the past 25 years
and continues to work for me now. I love that meditation while
bathing is so empowering, and I feel so blessed that it came into

my life at that time, that I recognized it, and that I applied it with diligence.

I would like to share my favorite closing meditation that is in the book *Heal Your Body.*

> *DEEP IN THE CENTER OF MY BEING, there is an infinite well of love. I now allow this love to flow to the surface. It fills my heart, my body, my mind, my consciousness, my very being, and radiates out from me in all directions and returns to me multiplied. The more love I use and give, the more I have to give; the supply is endless. The use of love makes ME FEEL GOOD. It is an expression of my inner joy. I love myself; therefore, I provide a comfortable home for myself, one that fills all my needs and is a pleasure to be in. I fill the rooms with the vibration of love so that all who enter, myself included, will feel this love and be nourished by it.*
>
> *I love myself; therefore, I work at a job that I truly enjoy doing, one that uses my creative talents and abilities, working with and for people whom I love and who love me, and earning a good income. I love myself; therefore, I behave and think in a loving way to all people, for I know that that which I give out returns to me multiplied. I only attract loving people in my world, for they are a mirror of what I am. I love myself; therefore, I forgive and totally release the past and all past experiences, and I am free. I love myself; therefore, I live totally in the now, experiencing each moment as good,*

and knowing that my future is bright, joyous, and secure. I am a beloved child of the universe, and the universe lovingly takes care of me now and forever more.

And so it is.

I love you

Reading this daily or as often as possible can truly assist you in changing your old destructive thoughts to thoughts that will create a healthier you, in mind, body, and spirit. We have the ability to create our own positive affirmations, depending on what we want to create in our lives moving forward.

Some of my daily mantras are:

My life is full of joy and abundance.

I am the power and authority in my life; I can create anything I want.

I am forgiveness, I am unconditional love, and I am peace.

I accept all experiences for my learning and my growth.

I am flexible; I go with the flow like a palm tree in the trade winds.

I digest every moment of every new day.

I am perfect and whole as I was created.

I release easily and comfortably anything not needed in my life at this time.

I am protected, I am safe, and all is well.

Gratitude, gratitude, gratitude.

CHAPTER 13

It was a Sunday afternoon in October 1997. We were up on Beaver Mountain at our condominium for the weekend. My brother Joe, his wife, Holly, and their four boys visited us for the day. General Conference, the semiannual meeting for members of the church, was held in Salt Lake City, and we were watching it on television. We had a nice dinner planned. Boyd and Tyler decided to go for a dirt-bike ride about noon and said they would be back in a couple of hours. We waited and waited and waited. As evening approached, Joe and Holly left to get back to St. George. I was with Trent and his friend Corey; they were about eight years old. We had planned to go home because of school and work the next day. I began to get really worried as darkness fell and Boyd and Tyler didn't return. I finally took the two boys on an ATV and went up the mountain to a cabin that people lived in all year long. Our neighbor said he would get in his truck and see if he could find them. I went back to the condo and put the boys to bed. It was a rough night! It wasn't until the next day at about two in the afternoon that search and rescue found Tyler and Boyd hiking out of the canyon. They were dirty, hungry, exhausted, and happy to be found!

They had ridden their bikes down into a place they could not get out of. I understood that it was quite an experience of perseverance and faith. I was full of emotion and had to resort to constant prayer to get through that. It had not been that long since I had lost Trevor. I felt that I could not go through another loss right now. What a relief that everything turned out all right!

My spiritual awareness began to grow tremendously after the loss of Trevor. I began a journey of spiritual growth, and because of the death that I had just experienced, I had a new level of understanding of life … and death.

On July 15, 1998, another tragedy hit our family. It had been a challenging day at work, and I remember feeling a little off. You are never prepared for any tragedy, certainly not for two so close. I was just learning to grieve for the loss of Trevor. Whatever the reason, the day seemed to be moving in slow motion. I picked up Trenton after work and dropped him off to meet Boyd and Tyler at Power Sports Authority, where Boyd worked. The three of them were going to the lake; Tyler was going to meet his friends, and Trenton was going with Boyd to show a boat. I went home to prepare dinner.

At about seven in the evening, I received a most disturbing call from Tyler's friend. I'll never forget that sinking feeling in my heart of total helplessness and fear when that phone call came. Kyle was in a panic, saying that Tyler had taken a hard fall and that the people on the boat were trying to revive him. Boyd got on the phone and was very distraught. He kept saying, "Not again, not again. What are we doing wrong?" He told me to meet him at the emergency room in the hospital. I thought I was dreaming and said, "This just can't be happening!"

Journal excerpt: July 15, 1998

Tyler had called about 4:30 asking me if Trent or I wanted to go to Gunlock Reservoir. Kyle his boss

would meet him there and teach him how to wake
board. Boyd had to show a boat, so I took Trent
into town and the 3 of them went off to the lake.
I came home after a long day at work and teaching
to do dinner and shower. I never saw Tyler again
alive; if I would have only known to put my arms
around him one last time and tell him how much
I loved him! You never know, though.

I called my neighbor Roxie and told her what had happened. She
came right away and took me to the hospital. I know I was in
shock when I arrived. I sat outside the door of the room where
Tyler was being treated, trembling with panic, fear and many
other conflicting emotions. Then I felt a calmness surround me,
as if someone were embracing me. I felt in my heart and heard
in my mind Trevor saying, "It is okay, Mom. Tyler and I get to
be together in order to move forward." I kept telling the doctors
and nurses that there was no use working on him. I told the nurse
that he wasn't going to stay here; he was moving forward with his
brother. I knew it and felt it with all my being! They worked on
him for three hours, to no avail.

Journal excerpt: July 16, 1998

This couldn't be happening! Why? It is not fair!
I already sacrificed one son; no, no, this is not
right. I am angry! My heart is again being ripped
out of my chest! The sorrow is so deep! We are
beginning another very spiritual experience, a
growing, learning, and another challenge. The
Stake Presidency (leaders) of the church in our
area came over tonight and gave me a special
blessing. It was a most beautiful blessing and I

felt the comforter descend upon me. From that point on I was strong and my feelings shifted from anger to faith and a certain joy of being the parent of two very special sons! I know this time what is ahead of me and oh how I wish I was way past it!

I was living the nightmare all over again. This time, I think, I knew how to handle grief better. When Trevor passed, I just didn't eat or sleep much, and I refused to take any medications. This time I forced myself to eat, and I did my tranquility breathing and meditation to sleep. I still would not use medications. I was stronger and I had experienced it only two years earlier with Trevor. But it really wasn't any easier. I just knew what to expect a little more. I worried about Trenton, my youngest boy. He was eight years of age and now had lost two brothers. I wondered often what was going through his young mind. I knew I had to be strong for him and be the best example of faith that I could. To this day he says it was because of the teachings of God's plan that he will see his brothers again, and his parents exemplifying a strong positive attitude, that he coped with the loss in a more positive way.

Again our friends and family rallied around us. They attempted to console and support us through another tragedy. People came into our lives that had experienced tragedy and wanted to be there to support us, people that I did not know or had never met. They knew what we were going through and wanted to be there for us. One couple lost two sons also; one of the boys committed suicide, and the other died from a rare blood disease. Listening to the stories of others who had lost their children made me realize even more how very blessed I was. There were others who had experienced worse. My heart was full of gratitude for each one of them for keeping our family in their prayers. I truly felt their prayers, and, as before, everyone began to go back to their own lives. I remember feeling that void again. I realized that it was time for me to take charge and hold my head high to the occasion.

Two sons in two years, practically to the day! No one would ever imagine such a thing. I grieved this unimaginable double loss, but my belief system gave me solace. I knew that I would see my sons again in another dimension, another time. I honored who they were, what they brought into my life, and what they taught me in their deaths. I held on to that. I believe nothing just happens. There is purpose in everything and everyone that comes into our lives. I learned so much from that experience and gained insight into life and death. It was when my true spiritual journey began. I will bow at the feet of my sons when I see them again, for giving of their physical existence, so that I could learn what I deserved to learn! I honor them and the memories of us together. They taught me so much in life and death. Gratitude for those things!

CHAPTER 14

Out of suffering have emerged the strongest souls.
—Kahlil Gibran

Relief Society is an organization for women in the Church of Jesus Christ of Latter Day Saints. I was sitting in a Relief Society class one Sunday, listening to a lesson on sacrifice. The word *sacrifice* can take on different meanings, I suppose, depending on your perspective. The teacher was talking about how we each choose to make sacrifices, small or large, every day; especially mothers do. She asked participants what sacrifices they made to become wives and mothers. There were various answers, such as putting off a college education, not being able to work, being tied down, and sacrificing their bodies to have babies. As I listened to these women coming from the perspective of a victim, I was compelled to speak up. If there was a time to share a small part of what I had learned from my experience of losing two boys, then this was the perfect opportunity. I proceeded, "We all have freedom of choice. You chose to be a mother and to be responsible for that choice. Yes, being a parent can be difficult, and, yes, it is one of the greatest opportunities to learn selfless love. I have to say that from my perspective, it has been my greatest blessing! My boys have taught me more than I could ever teach them.

They have been the source of my greatest sorrow and my greatest joy. I believe that one of the greatest discoveries of all time is that if people can change their minds and their attitudes, they can change the nature of any experience! I feel it is an honor to be a mother, and I thank my mother with all my heart for her attitude of gratitude that she exemplified for the experience of motherhood!"

My mother's wisdom and support were what assisted me through my difficult time. She was my rock, and I drew from her strength and her insight. My mother, El Marie Briggs Hansen Gunnell, had experienced challenges in her own life. She had lost a son, my brother, Billie, when he was eighteenth months old; she had been through a challenging divorce; she had just lost the love of her life, Franklin W. Gunnell; and now she had to watch her daughter go through this challenge. She not only grieved for her own loss of two grandsons but felt the pain of a daughter that she loved very much. My mother put her arms around me and said, "It is better to have had than to have never had before." With God by my side, the attitude of gratitude, and the knowledge that I could create whatever I wanted, I was able to turn my challenge into a positive experience and become more resilient than I was before. I knew it was time for me to honor the past, those things that I had learned. It was now time for me to release those things that had no purpose in my life at this time. The easy thing to do would be to slip into the "poor me" or victim role, to withdraw into my world and not think about who loved me and was concerned for me. That gets old real fast for everyone. I had gone to my sons' gravesite several times to honor them, and I always left sad. I finally said to myself, "They wouldn't want me sad. They are not even there anyway. I'm sure they are busy moving forward into the eternities, and I certainly don't want to hold them back!" So I quit going all the time; I felt they would want it that way too.

Journal excerpt: September 29, 1998

I have put off writing about my feelings because it just brings all my emotions to the surface, but I know it is necessary for my posterity to know of my feelings after going through such a loss. It would be easy to fall into that "poor me" or "unfair to me" mode. I can see how people could get consumed with such sadness, but we all have choices and I CHOOSE not to be a poor me! I'm so thankful for the things that I have been taught and the understanding of life after death. I know in my heart that Tyler and Trevor are together and someday I will be with them again. We will all be together again, but for now I love life and I want to live it to the fullest! I want to continue to learn and experience what I need to. I want to touch the lives of others, those in need of my insight. Trenton is my focus now and my joy! The funeral for Tyler was so nice and of course we had a coming together of friends and family that was unbelievable! How blessed we are to have such wonderful support! That definitely helps take you through a very difficult time with all the thoughts and prayers from so many!

All of us have challenges that come into our lives. We can't always choose what they are, but we can choose how we handle them. Releasing is the most important step, in my opinion, to be able to move forward in your life. I grew leaps and bounds in so many ways, and I was now ready to move forward! As a result of my choice, God and the universe blessed me with opportunities to inspire and uplift others. Because of my background and love for people, my nursing and my fitness and wellness coaching were avenues to do this. As time went on, other avenues presented themselves, and it took courage to follow them.

Tyler John 10, Trenton Boyd 2 months & Trevor Chase 8

Tyler John 17

Trevor Chase 13

Bonnie Lee as Celine Dion

Bonnie Lee as Celine Dion

Bonnie & Mark Engagement 2009

Bonnie Scuba Diving 2009

Bonnie and Trent - January 2011
Missionary Homecoming

Bonnie & Mark Sunset in Bali 2013

Yoga in Bali 2013

SECTION 3

CREATE THE FUTURE

CHAPTER 15

Life isn't about finding yourself, life is about
creating yourself.
                                    —George Bernard Shaw

Celine Dion inspires many through her music. I often played
her music in my exercise classes, and my boys and I would sing
"Because You Loved Me" in the car all the time. At Trevor's
funeral the Anderson girls, Jamie and Andrea (good friends of
the boys), sang that song beautifully and dedicated it to Trevor.
It was very touching. Two years later, Jamie and Andrea sang the
song from the movie *Titanic*, "My Heart Will Go On," at Tyler's
funeral and dedicated it to him. Those two songs took on personal
meaning to me.

The thing that is so interesting to me is that everywhere I went
people commented on how I resembled Celine Dion. The chefs in
the kitchen at Green Valley were in charge of our Christmas party
that year. They came to me and asked me to impersonate Celine
and lip-synch "My Heart Will Go On," because it was the song
of the year. With the encouragement from family and friends and
knowing that it would be something fun, exciting, and uplifting
for me, I decided to go for it!

I bought a beautiful "Celine Dion" gown, wig, and brown contacts. My friend who owned a Merle Norman salon assisted me with my makeup. I had to accentuate the characteristics that made me look like Celine, and she did an awesome job. Even *I* thought that I resembled her when I was in costume!

So I had created the look, and now I had to learn the song and practice the movements. I repeatedly watched a Celine Dion video. I practiced lip-synching the song over and over. It took my mind off the loss of my boys, and I wanted that during this holiday season. As the party date approached, I couldn't sleep because I was so nervous! My ego-mind kept saying, *What are you doing? Everyone is going to laugh at you! This is so stupid! You don't look like Celine. What are you trying to prove?* This is where I began to build my courage and let the ego-mind go.

The holidays are always difficult when there is such a void in your life. I just knew that this would take my mind away from the grief and give me something positive to think about. The music was therapy! It took me a while before I could sing "My Heart Will Go On" without my eyes welling up in tears. I watched how Celine moved, and I practiced again and again. I found it wasn't too difficult, and it seemed to come natural for me. She was known for her ballads, and she just had a few powerful stances and arm movements. The famous "hit the chest" was her signature move.

The Green Valley Christmas party was approaching. I was so nervous but excited too. The anticipation built day by day, until the time arrived. It took me all afternoon to get ready. I wanted everything to be perfect. I have to admit—I looked pretty great! I remember taking Trent to my brother's house to spend some time. They raved about my look, and I began to feel like Celine.

Boyd took me to the country club in Bloomington Hills for the big event.

Meanwhile, at the country club, things were being set up for my grand entrance. As I said before, Green Valley hosted celebrities on a regular basis, so when they announced that a special celebrity was coming to sing a few songs, it was very believable. The movie *Titanic* was a huge hit, and the theme song, "My Heart Will Go On," was playing on the radio constantly. Celine was everywhere in the media.

I will never forget the reaction of the crowd when I walked in. I have to admit, I was shaking from my toes to my fingers! The adrenaline was pumping pretty darn fast through my system. I had come this far and knew I had to overcome my fear and go with the plan. As I started to lip-synch "My Heart Will Go On," my knees became weak, and my hand holding the microphone was shaking so bad that I had to support it with my other hand, clasping it firmly before I lost it. I felt as if I were in a dream as I looked around and saw all of my coworkers and friends enjoying my performance as Celine Dion. I finished my song and felt that it had impacted the audience in a positive way. I realized how cool it was to uplift and inspire through music and felt a small part of what Celine surely feels all the time. The response from the audience was very positive. My own fitness instructors didn't recognize me; people actually thought that I was Celine Dion. It was an unbelievable experience. I loved it!

That very first night after I performed, I awoke with the urge to write Celine a letter expressing my feelings of gratitude for her inspiration. I felt this had come into my life at the perfect time! I wrote a four-page letter to her. My pen flowed on the paper. It was great therapy for me to write. I didn't know what to do with it after I wrote it, so I just tucked it away. I knew one day I would meet Celine. I didn't know how or when, but I knew.

I thought impersonating Celine would be just a one-time opportunity, but no. It was such a hit that I was asked to do six more Christmas parties that holiday. Word began to spread about the Celine Dion impersonator in town. This really was a blessing to me. The opportunity to forget my sorrow and spread joy through music was my healer. My heart was full of gratitude for this opportunity to come into my life.

Happy New Year, 1999! I had made it through the holidays. Life goes on after a tragedy, even if our hearts and minds don't think it should. What would this year bring? I started something that I felt was part of my destiny. It was my unique contribution to the energy of the universe. It was something I couldn't turn my back on. Celine had opened a door for me, and I chose to walk through that door. Doors open and close all the time. Our challenge is to have the discernment, wisdom, and insight to go through those doors that move us to our personal development and evolution. I discovered what it is like to be in alignment with my purpose. Opportunities flowed into my life!

For the first few years, every time someone called and asked that I perform, I wanted to say no and make up an excuse why I couldn't. I had to push myself through that ego-mind of mine. I made myself say, "Yes, I'd love to!" With every performance I became more and more courageous. It really taught me to let the ego-mind go and not to worry what other people thought. It was more important for me to let my heart lead the way. I had a passion to inspire and uplift others, and this was my opportunity to do that through music. What ended up being something that was motivated by giving to others became my greatest healer.

I learned so much about courage. Life takes courage. It is so easy to fall into a comfort zone and allow fear to stop us from living life fully. I'm thankful that I pushed myself out of that comfort zone, for it opened doors of opportunity and experiences that have enriched my life tremendously.

As the New Year began, I found myself onstage at all sorts of private parties, conventions, and fundraisers. My brother-in-law was in the National Guard. He asked me if I would learn another song and invited me to perform at the Military Awards Banquet. So I learned "Because You Loved Me." Now I had two special songs to share. The very two songs that was so special to my boys and to me. They were the songs that were sung at Tyler's and Trevor's funerals.

CHAPTER 16

That spring I got a phone call from Russ Terry, an agent of
Celebrity Doubles. A woman who had seen me at a convention
in St. George told him about me. This was so exciting! I felt I
had been discovered. He flew me to Salt Lake City for one of
his events. It was the beginning of many more events with Russ.
He told me that he thought I was a mirror image of Celine and
that it would serve me to learn to sing live, that I would make
better money. I think my first thought was, *"Are you crazy?"* After
thinking about it for a while, I asked myself, *"Why not?"* I used to
play my guitar and sing with my sister in high school, and I always
wanted to sing with a band. In the back of my mind, it really was
something that I always wanted to do, and I thought it would be
so much fun. I started voice lessons, and I took group lessons,
but I could see that it wouldn't be fast enough for me. I couldn't
make the progress that I needed to. People wanted me to perform,
and I had an urgency to move fast. It was at that time that Trish
and Lloyd Mecham came into my life, to assist me with moving
forward in my new undertaking as a Celine Dion impersonator.

I feel that Trish was an angel that came into my life with this
purpose. She was one of the best vocal coaches I could have
had. Trish and Lloyd owned Westwind Music, a music store and
recording studio. They had been in the music business for years.

They had worked in Las Vegas and with other tribute artists. I dedicated myself to learning Celine's music. We broke down every phrase and learned her style, so that I could impersonate her with precision. I learned much about my voice. I have a big vocal range, but learning correct technique was a challenge. I truly had the passion to sing and share Celine's music. Music filled a void in my life, and I used it as an effective coping strategy. If I was fearful, anxious, restless, sad, happy, or filled with any other emotion, my music was always there for me!

Celine is known for her awesome voice. I knew that singing like her would be a challenge and that I could never be Celine, but she had opened a door for me to be the best I could be. To spread her amazing music, to uplift and inspire people, even if it was a fraction of what she did—I felt that this opportunity was given to me for some special reason. I began to sing with my own voice from that point on.

I continued to perform for the guests at Green Valley Spa. They seemed to enjoy it very much, and it was a way for me to practice at a small venue. Guests would ask all the time, "Have you met Celine?" My response was always the same: "Not yet, but I will!" I knew I would, I just knew it! At the time, Celine lived in Florida. As events played out, Celine moved to Las Vegas for her show at Caesars Palace. I met lots of people who had intentions of assisting me to meet her, but it never quite worked out. One day a woman from New York, Dr. Karen Franks, was in my water fitness class. She told me how much I looked like Celine. I laughed and told her that I was a Celine Dion look-alike. She said that she stayed at Caesars Palace often when she was in Las Vegas. She thought that her hair stylist, Zhane was Celine's hair stylist for her show every night. She gave me her stylist's telephone number and told me to call her. The number sat on my desk for about three months before I called and set an appointment.

Everybody deserves a very best friend in their life. I have been so rewarded with so many wonderful friends and appreciate the things that they each bring into my life, but Cindy and I have developed that best friend relationship. Cindy and I planned a girls' weekend. It included having my hair done by Zhane at the Venus Hair Salon. It was a high-class experience, and when we arrived we were escorted back to Zhane's station. As we got to know each other, I learned that she was Celine's hairdresser. Cindy told her my story of losing the boys and falling into the experience of being a Celine impersonator. I never asked her to hook me up with Celine. I just wanted to have a new friend. When we left I felt I had accomplished that. We developed a special friendship and stayed connected.

Fall of November 2005, I planned to go see Celine's concert at Caesars Palace. My friend and assistant Holly Wilkinson and I watched for tickets online because it was a constantly sold-out show. Holly assisted me with booking events and taking phone calls. She also went with me to events and took care of details that I couldn't. We had so much fun, and I appreciated her so much! One evening she called and said her husband had given her money to purchase concert tickets for her birthday. Holly finally found two tickets available on Sunday, November 27, seventh row, front and center! I told her that those were our tickets and that it was meant to be! We booked them, and I called Zhane and left a message that we were coming to see Celine's show and would love to see her before the show. I didn't hear back from her for a couple of days; it was Thanksgiving weekend. On Friday night after Thanksgiving, Holly called and was excited beyond excited! I had left Holly's phone number for Zhane, because I worked and didn't want to miss her call. Celine's personal assistant, Anna, had called Holly and left a message to have me at the box office half an hour before the show, and they would take me back to meet Celine!

I knew it! I always knew in my heart that I would meet her. I wrote it down over and over, knowing that the universe would put it together for me. God blesses me again and again. I told everyone that I would meet her one day, to have the opportunity to thank her for opening doors for me to inspire and uplift through sharing my talents.

I learned that, after meeting Zhane the first time, she told Celine my story. Celine told her to let her know the next time I was there, because she would love to meet me. When Zhane got my message that I was coming to the show, she called Celine. Celine put the wheels in motion; she contacted Anna to get us set up. We had to get a security clearance, which took a few days.

It is so fun to see how things play out. Life is truly an adventure! *Gratitude, gratitude, gratitude!*

Sunday, November 27, 2005, came. Holly and I left St. George around three thirty in the afternoon and arrived an hour later in Las Vegas. We went directly to Venus Hair Salon to meet up with Zhane. I think that she was really excited to be able to connect us. We visited and said we would see her later at the showroom. She would be there doing Celine's hair. Holly and I went to eat and shop for a few hours.

We were at the Caesars box office at eight o'clock, as instructed. There were several dozen people trying to see Celine, even bribing the security guards. It was quite the experience. One lady had come all the way from Europe with a picture of Celine; she thought it would get her in to meet Celine. It didn't.

We heard my name called. It was Anna and a big, good-looking bodyguard there to take us back to meet Celine. As we moved through Celine's quarters backstage, I started to get really excited! It was like a maze, and I was embracing every moment of the experience. Holly and I didn't really know what to expect. I thought we would be part of a meet-and-greet with other fans. To my delight and surprise, we were escorted directly to her living room inside her home within Caesars. It was attached to her makeup and dressing room. It was nicely furnished with white leather couches and chairs. Her dining room was off to the side, with a long glass table that could about fifteen to twenty people. It was beautiful!

As I sat there, I began to get that nervous feeling in my stomach. I had been so calm up to this time. I think reality was setting in. As she walked through the swinging door that connected the two rooms, it felt so surreal, so much like a dream. She looked like an angel, with a glow of light around her. Such charisma and wonderful energy! I felt it as we embraced in a heart-to-heart hug.

I was finally able to thank her for her inspiration, her music, and opening a door for me to do what I was doing. I told her what an honor it was to share her music and how it had been my healer. She responded, "It is people like you who inspire me. Thank you." She also commented that she could see how people thought that we looked alike. I presented her with a gift certificate to Green Valley Resort. She showered us with a bag of "Celine goodies": DVD, CDs, pictures, "A New Day Has Come" sweatshirt, perfume, etc. We sat on the white leather couch and held hands as we visited.

Holly bought a brand-new camera to take lots of pictures. When we were with Celine, the camera would not work. We tried several times; even Celine tried to get it to work, to no avail. She called in her personal photographer to take a few pictures of us. She autographed them and sent them to us a few weeks later. The interesting thing is that our camera worked fine after we left her quarters. I understood that I wouldn't have had a personalized, autographed photo of us if the camera had worked. I believe there are no coincidences; it was one of those blessings in disguise! We spent thirty or forty minutes with Celine. She is so heart-driven, so gracious and beautiful. It was an awesome experience. After our visit, her big, good-looking bodyguard escorted us back to our seventh-row, front-and-center seats. Let the show begin! The show was amazing. It most definitely was another moment in life to embrace.

Gratitude for this opportunity! God bless Celine in her journey of sharing and uplifting others!

Chapter 17

When you dedicate yourself to transforming your inner world, your life quickly shifts from the ordinary to the realm of the extraordinary.
—Robin Sharma

I was at the height of my "Celine" career, and my fiftieth birthday was upon me. I received a call to perform for a company party. This party would be held at the Staheli Farmhouse in the loft. It turned out to be something I did not expect. Let me share with you a story written about this event, by the sister of a friend who attended and was from the East Coast. He e-mailed me a copy.

> My brother has managed to finesse his way into a group of Mormons, which sounds like a rather "Duh" thing to say, since the entire state of Utah is Mormon, but if you knew Don you'd understand why I find this interesting. The fact of the matter is that my brother is the epitome of Mr. Personality. I don't believe he has an enemy on earth and can talk to anyone! Literally, the fact that he rides a Harley, and one of his closest Mormon pals there runs the Harley Davidson

Shop, probably is what got the Mormon ball rolling, but ... I'm digressing again. Don's friend, named Boyd, his wife, named Bonnie, is a Celine Dion Impersonator, and a very good one. Bonnie looks quite a bit like Celine and her act is rather amazing! At any rate, Bonnie was turning 50 while we were there so a big Mormon Birthday Party had been planned and Jeannie and I were invited.

I could not help wondering what a Mormon birthday party would be like. It was a surprise ... Bonnie thought she was being hired to perform at someone else's party. So, we went hither and yon, all around the St. George, Utah area until we ended up on a dairy farm out in the middle of ... well ... somewhere, I guess, but I could not find my way back again if you offered me a million!

Aside from the barn full of cows, we climbed some stairs that lead up over a barn-like structure to a huge open air loft where a country band was wailing away and a Mormon feast had been laid out on two long picnic tables. There were two punch bowls full of ice water and lemon slices (no booze of course) and just about every sort of dessert you could imagine! Mormons like desserts! People were singing, dancing, and laughing and greeting each other and Jeannie & I were greeted as well, but I am not very good with names. I doubt that I could repeat any of them! It was a pretty wild affair, if laughter and LOUD music qualifies as "wild" ... but the best was yet to come. In the midst of all this commotion, Bonnie arrived in her Celine Dion get-up, thinking she was there to perform for someone else. She was all slinky and clad in body-fitting white spandex with big hair and marvelous moves and while I was watching her perform, which she did extremely well, I could not help thinking that this was the oddest and most memorable birthday party that I had ever attended! We were up in an open air loft over a barn, music blaring, Celine Dion was singing, and the aroma of dairy cows wafted through the scene like magical fog. One can only sigh …

I could only laugh out loud. I sang for my own birthday party!

Exciting things continued to open up for me to be involved in. I was asked to open for "The Jets" on New Year's Eve, First Night celebration in southern Utah. I also got invited to the Aladdin Hotel in Vegas to perform with Cirque du Soleil for a convention of eight thousand people. An awesome experience! Trish Mecham, my vocal coach, went with me. I was so glad to have her support. We arrived at the Aladdin Hotel and they treated me like royalty from the start. We had a gorgeous suite for two nights and access to the executive suite, where all the food and drinks were complimentary. When we walked through the doors of the showroom, we both gasped at the sight. There was Cirque du Soleil on the stage, practicing their routine. I was going to perform with one of the top acts in Vegas! Wow! The sound check went amazingly well. I sounded so great that I couldn't even believe that it was me. The showroom was beautiful and big, and the dressing room was huge. Trish and I looked at each other and just cracked up. I was so naive about all of this. God was really showing me what we can create with some passion and determination. They recorded me with five cameras, and I got a great promotional DVD out of it. It was a night to remember!

Legends in Concert, Las Vegas, contacted me to be involved with a photo shoot for Universal Studios in Japan. I spent three days in Vegas at the Imperial Palace Hotel. I had so much fun, and I met some awesome impersonators; Michael Jackson, Madonna, Ricky Martin, Stevie Wonder, Whitney Houston, Janet Jackson, Prince. We made a video and took lots of shots for posters that would be seen all over Japan. I got voted the impersonator that looks most like her celebrity without any makeup. I made some new friends and made some great contacts for the future.

I received a call from the St. George Recreation Center regarding an opportunity to perform for the National Girls Softball teams, from all over the United States. There were 148 teams, coaches, and their families and friends. The girls were ages ten through seventeen. There were over six thousand people in the Burns Arena. The plan was for Boyd to drive me in on a Harley, through the crowd, and up to the stage. I would run up the stairs and break out into the song "I Drove All Night." This was the entrance that I had used several times before; it was always very effective. They never said that I was Celine Dion but announced that a diva from Las Vegas was arriving to perform. I really felt like Celine that evening! The crowd surrounded me and almost pulled me off the motorcycle. Once I was onstage, all the people were calling, "Celine, Celine, we love you, Celine," and climbing up on the stage. I couldn't believe it. The crowd was going wild! After I finished my show, security had to protect me from the crowd. I jumped on the Harley, and away we went with fans running after me. It was quite the event, one I certainly will remember forever.

Doors continued to open for me, and I traveled to Los Angeles quite a bit to perform for my sister Melody and her Champions for Children Charity Red Carpet Events.

Journal excerpt: May 25, 2006

> Flew to L.A. this morning and Melody picked me up. It is her big kick-off event for Pocket Nutrition and Champions for Children Charity. The charity is sponsored by Ken Norton, the boxing heavyweight champion. I had a great weekend! I sang "I'm Alive" and "I Drove All Night." The audience loved it! That is just what I wanted to hear!! Through one of these events I met David Sherry, who was a Neil Diamond tribute artist from San Diego. We will do several events together in the coming years. He invited me to be his guest and open for him at his show at the AVO Playhouse Theater in Vista, California.

Journal excerpt: June 12, 2006

> I flew in early this a.m. to L.A. and Mel picked me up. We had an event in Hollywood at a mansion where they were doing a fundraiser. Mary Colver, of the motion picture council, wanted me to perform as Celine. I sang the song "I'm Alive." It was outdoors on the most beautiful day, on the most beautiful grounds surrounding a huge mansion home of "Old Hollywood" area. You only see places like that in the movies! It was a successful performance, and after we left and headed for San Diego where I met David

at the AVO Playhouse Theater for sound check. I opened his show with "I'm Alive." While he changed between songs I sang, "That's the Way It Is," and we sang the duet "You Don't Bring Me Flowers." It was so much FUN! What a great weekend!

David and I became great friends and had the opportunity to perform several more shows together. I arranged for us to to do a fundraiser for the musical theater. I brought David from California and he and I put on a show, "Neil and Celine." Our two scheduled shows sold out. We had to add a third night, which sold out too. It was a fun place to do a show, because of all the extra stage props that we had available. A couple of the highlights: I opened the show entering on a Harley-Davidson motorcycle, I sat in a swing as I sang, and then I stood on the bow of a ship resembling the *Titanic*. It was such a blast. Everyone in the audience seemed to have such a great time, and we were able to raise a fair amount of money for the theater.

I also lined up a Neil Diamond and Celine Dion show at Sun River Community that sold out in a few hours, and performances for several conventions at the Convention Center. I always enjoyed performing with David; he had such a passion for what he did and was very good at it. I felt that we inspired each other.

The dream of a tribute artist is to meet the celebrity whom they represent. David expressed how much he desired to meet the real Neil Diamond. I shared with him my story of how I met Celine, and I know that the law of attraction came into play for me. I thought it, I believed it, I felt it, I visualized it, I wrote it down, and I created it with my genie in the bottle. He looked at me and said, "Really? I'm going to do that!" Guess what? He did, and a few years later he shared with me the awesome experience of meeting Neil Diamond. The law of attraction works!

I attended the Reel Awards, which was the "Academy Awards" of impersonators," held at the Hollywood Roosevelt Hotel in Hollywood, California. That was an experience! Impersonators from all over the world arrived in limousines, and they walked the red carpet surrounded by paparazzi trying to get a glimpse and a picture of a star or two. They had live performances by some of the best and gave awards. I sat with impersonators of Tiger Woods, Jay Leno, Whitney Houston, Jerry Lewis, and Tina Turner. It was an evening full of interviews, networking, and making new friends. It was at this time I decided I would take French lessons, because there were so many journalists that were speaking to me in French. There were reporters from all over the world. The cameras were flashing, and I really was able to feel what it was like to be a celebrity. I must say I loved every minute of it!

I continued to have all kinds of bizarre experiences with people thinking that I was Celine. I bought a Chrysler 300C and had "CELINE" license plates on the back of it. That gave people something to talk about! Celine had done a marketing campaign for Chrysler, and she sang "I Drove All Night." I can't tell you how many times people would pull up to the side of me while I was driving and think I was Celine. They would snap pictures and follow me! One day I actually had to lose a car that was following me. It was interesting that in my community of St. George, rumors began to fly that Celine had a house there, and there were constant sightings of Celine everywhere. I had to laugh; I knew I was stirring things up a little. I did all kinds of events, private parties, weddings, trade shows, and conventions.

I was asked to participate in a humanitarian entertainment group that went to Ireland for ten days. I decided to take my mother with me, so that we could have some special time together. It was a wonderful time to share together. There were thirty of us on the bus, all ages and all types of acts. It was an awesome experience going into senior citizen centers, children's hospitals, and orphanages to share our talents. They love Celine Dion, and I was well received by the Irish people. We also got to partake of the Irish culture. Oh, those beautiful green rolling hills with daffodils that grow wild and of course the Irish pubs! We kicked our heels up almost every night doing the Irish jig. We marched in the St. Patrick's Day Parade in Dublin, with the American Legion. Mom was so thrilled when they asked her to carry the American flag! It was bigger than she was, but she waved that flag with American pride. We toured the awesome castles of old and learned the history of that country that goes back to AD 400 or 500. Our guide shared many old tales of the castles there in Ireland. My favorite was the tale of the Blarney Stone at the Blarney Castle.

The old tale goes like this, as I remember. In the day of witch hunts, if you were suspected of being a witch, they would throw you in the river. If you drowned, you were not a witch, but if you survived, you were a witch and would be burned at the stake. The story goes that a prince that lived in the Blarney Castle had a speech impediment, possibly a severe lisp. One day he was looking over the river down below and saw a woman crying for help, for she would surely drown! The prince, being a kind man, rushed to save her, not knowing that she was suspected of witchcraft. He did save her, and because of that the woman granted him one wish. He wished that his speech would be perfect and that he would have the "gift of gab." The woman picked up a stone and said, "Kiss this stone and you will be granted perfect speech and the gift of gab." The prince kissed the stone, and he was healed! He was so overcome with joy that he took the stone high to the top of the Blarney Castle and cemented the stone into the castle wall, where it would stay forever. So the story goes that if you kiss this stone, you are granted the gift of gab. We hiked to the top, about 250 steps, lay on our backs, hung our heads out over the wall, and kissed the stone. I got double the gift of gab, because they made me kiss it twice! Why? Because they didn't get a picture the first time!

I was invited to another event in The Lakes, Las Vegas. I was asked to emcee a fashion show right on the water, where they had a floating bridge. Many events were held at that venue; it is a beautiful place. This is where Celine has a Las Vegas home. I was excited to be a part of it. I had gotten an amazing long, curly wig to wear for my Celine impersonations. It was so much easier to put on a wig than to try and do my own hair. I used it a couple of times, and it worked like a dream. This particular day was very windy, and as I began to sing the song "I'm Alive," a gust of wind almost took that wig right off my head! I put one hand on my head to hold the wig in place and held the microphone in my other hand. I had to make a quick decision. Either keep my hand on the top of my head for the rest of the song or pull the wig off, hair net and all. So I pulled it off, looked at the sound man, and threw the wig at him, saying, "Hold this!" My own hair fell softly down over my shoulders. He was shocked, to say the least, along with the entire audience. I yelled, "Whooo hooo, I'm alive!" The audience roared with laughter. I booked two events from that performance.

Another time, I was asked to perform at the Ritz-Carlton in The Lakes, Las Vegas, for a convention. My friend Craig, whom I had met at one of my previous performances, was in charge of the entertainment for this event and wanted me as "Celine." Of course, I had my bodyguards and my personal assistant with me; this always adds to the ambiance. My bodyguards did a sweep through the audience to give the impression that someone of very high profile was to be there. The excitement and the energy continued to build. They kept me in the back as Craig announced, "We have a special guest to entertain you tonight. Someone you all know who lives right here in The Lakes, Las Vegas. This entertainer's show has been dark this week, so many of you were disappointed when you could not see her show. This is a very special occasion, and would you please welcome this very special guest!" They began to play my introductory music, and I walked out singing, "I'm Alive." I'll never forget the response from the audience. The crowd was in awe! Camera flashes started going off, people were on their cell phones calling their families and friends, holding the phones up so they could hear.

I always felt that once I started singing, the fans would know that I was a tribute artist and not the real Celine, but I was surprised more often than not at the crowd's response. This crowd was getting into the whole experience of it, and it was great! After I sang "My Heart Will Go On," they asked me to walk around to meet and greet. As I did this, some comments such as, "Oh, Celine, I love your music," "Oh, Celine, thank you for being here tonight," and "Oh, Celine, I have all of your albums," made me realize that they thought I was the real Celine! I looked at Craig, not really knowing if I should continue this charade, and he whispered in my ear, "You're doing awesome. Play it out girl, play it out!" I laugh at the situation now, knowing that he loved seeing the response of the crowd. The show was such a big success, he tipped me an extra thousand dollars! Later when I spoke to Craig, he said that 90 percent of the people still thought that I was the real Celine. He thanked me again for the wonderful time it was for all who were there. Times like this made it so rewarding to do what I did!

When I was in Las Vegas, it was pretty common for people to come up to me on the streets and in restaurants, thinking that I was Celine Dion. I would say, "Oh no, I'm not Celine." Noticing the look of disappointment on their faces, I added, "But I'm a Celine impersonator." They would say, "That's the next-best thing. Can we have a picture with you?" My agent told me to carry on the charade, representing Celine in a manner of utmost respect. I always had such admiration for Celine, who she was, and what she represented that nothing else ever entered my mind. So that is what I did, realizing that it uplifted and gave people something exciting to talk about. It was a big part of the fun for all of us!

I remember receiving a call from Tony Strike, who was our senior class president at East High School. It was our thirtieth class reunion. Tony invited me to show up as Celine and perform. He gave quite the introduction, of how he had connections in Las Vegas and was able to bring in a special celebrity. I was backstage listening to this, feeling more and more nervous, more nervous than I had ever experienced. I actually wanted to throw up! I could see in my mind all my high school classmates, friends, cheerleaders, and athletes. I think I had flashed back in my mind to those good ol' insecure high school days. As my music began, I walked out onstage, and as I began to sing, I looked out at everyone in the audience and said to myself, "Who are all these old people! I don't know any of them!" I calmed right down and gave them a performance to remember. I laugh about that experience often! The thoughts we harbor from the past … very interesting!

Performing had gotten into my blood. I began to get more and more comfortable with it. I decided that it was time to develop my website www.iamaliveproductions.com. That name was so perfect for how I felt, I am Alive! I was truly thankful for this opportunity that had come into my life and knew this was an opportunity to give back to society in a way that was also healing for me. After losing my boys, there was a void in my life and now I could fill that void with something positive, I knew it, and I felt it!

Opportunities to share my story of loss, and developing my "Celine act", came into my life often. I was asked to contribute to the book, "Thinking About Tomorrow" by Susan Crandall. Also, ELAN magazine and other publications. I participated in several media shows and spoke at many events, always sharing my story and often using Celine's music. It was very fulfilling for me, and I knew it was a story meant to be shared.

CHAPTER 18

Courage is not the absence of fear, but rather the
judgment that something else is more important
than fear

—Ambrose Redmoon

I know how much I grew in courage, confidence, and determination
at that time, and I continue to grow now. One of the motivations
for me was to be an example of strength to my surviving son,
Trent. After the loss of Trevor and Tyler, it would have been
so easy to withdraw into fear. Actually, I had begun to do just
that! It was my music and meditative techniques, not doctors or
medications that empowered me to overcome severe anxiety. I
was willing to discipline myself to do what it takes to overcome. I
was filled with fear of losing someone else close to me, or even my
own life. I knew where my comfort zone was and wanted to stay
in it. I had a hard time driving my car for any distance. I drove
to work and back home, and only when it was daylight. Anxiety
attacks are no fun. My heart would begin to race, my eyes went
blurry, and I became dizzy, as if I would pass out. I know what it
feels like to be consumed with fear.

I was in a bookstore in Salt Lake with my mother and sister. I
had been struggling with anxiety for quite some time. As I looked

around the store, a book jumped out at me, *Life without Limits* by Lucinda Bassett. It was not a coincidence. I opened it to the exact page that changed me. It was the author's story of fighting anxiety herself that made me realize fear was the basis of my anxiety and that I could change things through my thoughts. This book connected me with that which I had learned from the monks at Green Valley.

The Tibetan monks' Eastern philosophy taught me about the value of vibration from sound; the chanting that they do is so powerful. So, when my attacks would come on, I would begin to sing or hum my favorite tune. I realized that my mind was creating highly unlikely situations. I learned to overcome my "monkey mind" by chanting and learning to breathe a tranquility breath. No drugs! I also would repeat my positive affirmations over and over: "I am the power and authority in my life!" *Awesome*!

I continued to seek ways to build courage. My opportunity impersonating Celine really assisted with that. Have faith in God and have faith in yourself, learning not to worry about the things you cannot control. Life happens, and when you "let go and let God," life is so much easier! This is why when people would ask, "You don't let Trent water ski, do you?" my reply has always been, "Absolutely, if he chooses. It is his journey to create. I will not put fear into him. He deserves to live a life of courage, to experience those things he desires. No fear!" I want to teach him this through my example. Life takes courage!

Musical theater became part of my life, since I had friends that encouraged me to audition for *South Pacific*. This gave me the chance again to leave my comfort zone and try something new. I had so much fun! I was cast as the head nurse, Nellie's friend. The music and dance were great; I was hooked. The next show

I auditioned for was *Man of La Mancha*. It was a very deep, emotional drama. I remember getting goose bumps every time we did the finale, "To Dream the Impossible Dream."

During the auditions for *Man of La Mancha*, I was going through some personel challenges, and I wasn't going to participate, but my sweet friend Bridget encouraged me. She knew that it would be a great thing for me. Bridget set up a private audition with the director, because I had been out of town at an event performing. When we showed up at the theater, the director was waiting. He informed us that there were several parts available. He said that there was a scene in the play that had two horses in it, and these horses did a fun dance. As we left the theater, I looked at Bridget and said, "He better not cast us as horses, or I'm not going to be in this one." I did not want to be a horse!

The director cast us as ensemble, which included several parts, mostly wenches in the dungeon. As I learned more about this story, and the play started to come together, I became more and more excited to be a part of it. It was at our third rehearsal that the director looked right at Bridget and me and said, "Bridget, you will be the horse, and, Bonnie, you will be the horse's ass." I went white! I had attracted it because I said I didn't want it! That was the Law of Attraction at work! That is the law of the universe that says you create what you think about and I was thinking that I did not want to be that! In my mind, I was Bridget's rear end under a blanket. It turned out that she wore a beautiful horse head, and I wore a donkey head, with lots of personality! Yes, we did a little dance that was so much fun. I actually loved livening the whole scene up. It really fit me, being the "horse's ass!"

My sweet mother has always been my cheerleader. She was thrilled that I had made the cuts for the play. When she asked me what part I was playing, I giggled and told her that I had gotten the part of the horse's ass. After a moment's silence, my wonderfully positive mother said, "How wonderful! Did you know that the horse's rear end is the most beautiful and powerful part of the whole horse?" Coming from a woman who raised horses and loved them, that was an awesome perspective! That story will go down in history at the St. George Musical Theater archives. We laughed about that through the whole production.

The final production that I was in was "Singin' in the Rain." I was cast as the diva. It was such an uplifting play. I loved everything about it: the music, the dance, and my fellow cast members. I always made such great friends at the theater. They were all so talented. It was definitely another place for me to surround myself with music and positive people, which I believe assisted me to heal.

I learned so much from being in the theater. I loved every minute of it! I am so thankful that I took that opportunity.

CHAPTER 19

The happiness you feel is in direct proportion to
the love you give.

—Oprah Winfrey

So many times in Bali, I had memories come up that took me
back to my time in Peru with my son Trent. Bali, like Peru
is a beautiful country with an interesting history, culture, and
people. There were many similarities: such as despite the poverty
they seemed so happy and the people were so hard-working and
generally humble.

I watched Trent blossom into a wonderful young man. He was
working hard on receiving his Eagle Scout award. The scouting
program always played an important part in the lives of my boys.
All three of them were presented the Eagle award. Sometimes an
opportunity comes up to provide an experience of a lifetime, one
that will change your life forever. We had that chance come into
our lives. We were invited to participate in a trip to Peru with a
humanitarian program, Eagle Condor Humanitarian. This group
was created by a great friend that had served a mission in Peru for
the Church of Jesus Christ of Latter-day Saints and fell in love
with the country and the people. He wanted to assist them in
moving forward to create small businesses for economic growth.

Trent decided that for his final big Eagle project he would put together a hundred hygiene kits to take into the small communities, so he could teach them good hygiene. These kits consisted of toothbrushes, toothpaste, shampoo, conditioner, soap, and lotion. We put these supplies into quart-size baggies. Items that seem so ordinary to us seemed foreign to the people we would be working with. It surprised me that good hygiene was not practiced in these villages. They had never been taught to brush their teeth, at least not the way we brushed our teeth. We also gathered clothes, learning supplies, and books. The plan was to go into communities, orphanages, hospitals, and private homes to assist them with whatever their needs were. We handed out the health kits, books, and clothes, built bathrooms, laid foundations for community centers, painted the buildings at schoolhouses and orphanages, played with the children, and dug wells. Digging a well was the most physically difficult thing that I have ever done in my life! There were six to eight of us in the hole, each with a shovel in hand. The earth was so hard that I was lucky if I got any dirt at all. We dug and dug and barely got anywhere. Who knew? I didn't have any idea that it was so difficult to dig a well! I told my "peeps," "Take a picture of this one. I doubt you'll ever see me in a hole, digging a well ever again!"

They are very hard workers and were right beside us as we worked for the benefit of their homes and communities. We spent time in Cuzco, which I absolutely loved! It is almost twelve thousand feet high in the Peruvian Andes. When we arrived, they gave us cocoa tea for elevation sickness. There is so much history there; there are ancient ruins everywhere, and we had the opportunity to sight-see every other day. We went to Sacsayhuaman and Tambomachay Ruins overlooking Cuzco to start our trip.

Journal excerpt: Saturday, June 18, 2005

It was a work day in the community of Salkantay, 13,100 feet in elevation. It's the highest that we've been so far, you can feel the difference! It was quite the bus ride up—very primitive roads! Very windy and steep with drop-off cliffs. It would be an ATV road in my opinion. I was impressed with the bus driver and the bus! There was never any doubt we'd make it, I feel protected. It was a very primitive village. The people were so excited to see us! Boyd and I brought a sewing machine to donate and 100 battery-free flashlights. Trenton taught them how to use his health kits with a demonstration. Each family got one, two depending on the size of their family. It was so fun to watch him and be there to participate. We are so blessed to be able to hand-deliver these supplies to these sweet people! They are so humble and thankful for the chance to have help in improving their lifestyle. They are so used to tradition only, never leaving that comfort zone. We laid cement for a new community center, played with the kids, and had such a memorable experience.

A highlight was our visit to Machu Picchu Ruins at the top of the Peruvian Andes. It was a very spiritual atmosphere. I would call it amazing! The people treated us like celebrities as we went from village to village; they showed us their thanks by offering us the best that they had to give: a variety of potatoes that were cooked in the ground. We accepted them with gratitude. After all these wonderful experiences in Peru, we were changed forever! Our perspective on abundance was different. When we arrived back on American soil, everyone cheered and began to sing "God Bless America." I have never again taken the abundance that flows into my life for granted. Trent still says that the experience he had at seventeen years old in Peru was life changing for him. I'm so thankful that I had that awesome time spent in Peru with those wonderful people. I learned so much.

CHAPTER 20

Morality—To do what is right regardless of what others tell you.

Obedience—To do what you are told regardless of what you know to be right.

—Kristi Bek

I always taught my boys to honor who they were. When they left the house, I would say, "Remember who you are and what you stand for. Return with honor." I know that honoring who we are and honoring what we are becoming allows life to unfold before us in all its brilliance. Free will is God's plan, and we choose to bring heaven to our earth. Honoring who you are means to trust each choice that you make, knowing that there is always a consequence. For every action there is a reaction. Only your life can be the gift that you intended. We all have our own answers in our hearts. Take time to listen what your heart is saying. Know that every thought, word, and deed has an effect in the universe! We are all connected through energy. You breathe in and I breathe out, I breathe in and you breathe out.

My whole life to this point was to serve God, family, church, work, and community. As years go by, we all change; that is all we can depend on: change. We do evolve; it is a process. I had made a commitment in the Temple of the Church of Latter-day Saints in 1977 to strive toward an eternal marriage and family. That is what I was taught growing up in the Church of Jesus Christ of Latter-day Saints. Prophets told us that the purpose of life was creating an eternal family. To be married in the sacred temple there are certain requirements that have to be fulfilled: basic values of integrity, morality, service, attending regular church meetings, tithing, and donations to the church. I was raised that way, and it really is a big part of who I am. I believe integrity, and to be your word, is one of the most important values to live by. There are many values that are true, and living by those values creates positive consequences in our lives. I also believe that we have free will to choose how we honor God, a higher self or divine intelligence, whatever that looks like to each of us. I have expanded my beliefs and have grown so much spiritually knowing that through the wonderment of life and the experiences that we have, we move towards a better understanding of faith and God's plan. I choose to stay open, to follow my own heart and mind, being true to myself.

Looking back, I know that I did the best I could in our marriage. I understand now that it was important for Boyd to be part of my journey, so that I could learn so much about relationships, myself, and life. He was one of my greatest teachers! We had the blessing of three beautiful sons that filled our lives with true joy. A lot of people have asked me if losing our two sons contributed to the divorce. I have to say no, for me that was not the case. Yes, it was stressful to lose two sons two years apart and it was a great cross to bear. For many couples it could be the reason or excuse for a divorce, but for me it wasn't. Everyone grieves differently, and I can't speak for Boyd, but I honored that. I believe that when we lost Trevor it actually brought us together as a family, our extended family too. The loss of Tyler was more stressful on our family and a little more difficult, because I don't think that there was time enough to heal psychologically from losing Trevor. As I pulled every bit of faith that I had deep inside of me to survive this experience, I began to evolve and empower myself. I did have a choice how I would handle this challenge but in my mind the only way was to move forward in believing that this experience had purpose and that I was learning some extra-ordinary lessons! I was changing, I realized that Boyd and I were so different in so many ways and we had grown too far apart. Even without losing the boys our journey apart would have happened.

Journal excerpt: May 4, 2007

I know that I have created a life outside of my relationship for emotional survival. I realized none of us can put the responsibility on someone else to bring us happiness. That is our responsibility, ours alone. Others can bring wonderful things into our lives along the way, but true happiness is ours to discover. I've tried in my own way to contribute to the relationship, but I understand he is independent and who he is. I have just stuffed so many feelings for too many years! I've worn blinders because of my insecurities and tried to block out the hurt but my heart has shut down now.

I had evolved to a different place. I loved Boyd for the thirty years we had together and for being the father of my three sons, and I always will, but I wasn't in love with him. I knew in my heart that we both deserved different. I had prayed and meditated over the situation for several years, and when the timing was right, things fell into place. God blessed me, and I felt his arms around me once again in a situation that required courage if I wanted change in my life.

The most difficult thing that I ever had to do was to be honest with myself, and then act on the truth with Boyd. Leaving after thirty years of marriage took a lot of courage. I knew that there would be judgment. I had to hold my head high. I knew that I was sure of my decision. My soul told me that it was the right thing to do, no matter what others said. To this day, I have no regrets about the choices I have made in my past, to bring me to where I am today. I honor the past in every way. I've loved, I've lost, I've trusted, I've hurt, I've missed, I've made mistakes, but above all, I've learned!

After moving out, I felt a weight lifted off of me. I sensed a feeling of freedom! I moved forward staying busy with Green Valley Resort as their fitness director, evening manager at Planet Beach Spa, with musical theater, and with traveling doing my Celine impersonations. I created a variety of activities to fill the void in my life that divorce can create. I knew that if I did that instead of going to the victim space I would be a lot happier. So I surrounded myself with positive people, places, and things, so that I didn't get lonesome. On nights that I was at home alone, I would eat dinner and then go for a walk. I always loved my walks. They were an opportunity to clear my head, make calls to my mother or other family, and get some exercise. I always felt it was better to walk than sit on the couch, watching TV and eating bonbons. My sweet girlfriend Darci Hansen lived in my neighborhood. We walked often in the evenings and would share our dreams and our goals. Darci had a dream of having her own magazine for southern Utah. She had been writing as the social columnist for

St. George Magazine for a couple of years. She came to me and asked me if I would be on the board and participate in launching her new magazine, *Elan Woman*. I was so involved and busy at the time, I wasn't sure if I could handle one more thing. I asked her what élan meant, she told me that it meant life expression, spirit, vigor and enthusiasm. I knew at that moment it was meant for me to be involved! It proved to be an amazing experience working with such talented and extraordinary women. I was the social columnist, covering all the great events that came to southern Utah. Thank you, Darci, for including me in this wonderful project and dream of yours, at a time when it really served me!

Chapter 21

The greatest gift you will ever receive is the gift of loving and believing in yourself. Guard this gift with your life. It is the only thing that will truly be yours.

—*Tiffany Loren Rowe*

It was a beautiful Bali morning, six o'clock. It was still dark as I stumbled my way to the residence of a Hindu yogi, but the early birds were singing and I could feel and smell the crispness in the air. I had the opportunity to start this new day with a kundalini yoga class. This special place was surreal. I love yoga for the mind, body, and spirit connection that it can offer any of us. This practice originated in India, almost 26,000 years ago and is an integral part of the Hindu religion. I thought that it would be the perfect place to experience a yoga class. I was in Bali, and there definitely was the energy of peace and love. I think of how this spiritual awareness began with me, and I know I always had it to a certain degree, but after I lost my boys and had been through a divorce, I was eager to absorb more.

After my divorce I began to take relationship workshops and empowerment courses for self-improvement. I had been studying Eastern philosophy, focusing on mind, body, and spirit, since I lost the boys. I realized how grateful I was for having been taught basic gospel principles in my youth, through my parents, church, and personal study of Scriptures. I had a foundation to build upon. I was on this path of self-discovery. I thirsted for all the information I could find, from Deepak Chopra, Eckhart Tolle, Wayne Dyer, Caroline Myss and many more. I took Trenton with me for his high school graduation present, to a program called Impact Trainings; we did the course together. Impact training is a world class training company, focusing on assisting people get the most out of their lives. My brother Joe had done the program and shared what he learned with me. It sounded awesome! Impact training pulled everything together for me that I had been learning through self-study. Trenton loved it too, and it brought us very close.

The training program was presented with the intention of not just listening to someone speak but actually having the opportunity to experience the concept that was being taught. Through all kinds of various exercises and experiences, we were able to internalize certain principles and how they worked. We had to be teachable and be willing to make changes in our thoughts and in our lives. Probably one of the first things that I learned to apply was to be open to all possibilities. We were taught the Law of Attraction and looking back, I realize now that I used that principle to bring forth my meeting of Celine Dion.What you think about is what you create in your life. I love the whole concept of how so very powerful each of us is. We have the ability to create whatever we want.

We learned that everything is energy, and everything has a vibration. Depending on that vibration, reactions to it are created. For example, let us take communication and words. Normally, someone comes up to you and says, "You *have* to," or "You *should* do that," or "You *need* to do this." How does that make you feel? Do you feel a little defensive? The low-vibration words get a low-vibration response! *Should* or *need* create a defensive reaction. In working with people, high-energy words would be "You *get* to, you *deserve* to, or this would *serve* you." Another example is "I want to *help* you." The word *help* comes from ego, and the other person comes away with a feeling of owing you, while the person "helping" gets their ego boosted. Try this instead: "I want to *assist* you." You are *assisting* them to empower themselves. With this slight change in communication approach, watch how people respond to you. They might think you talk funny for a while, but they will eventually respond to you in a more positive way.

I felt that it was important to work on my spirituality, my relationship with God, and to discover who I really was. "I am a radiant, enthusiastic, inspiring spirit of light. My purpose is to spread unconditional love, passion, and peace, through being a radiant, enthusiastic, inspiring spirit being of light in gratitude for all that is. While creating a world of joy, abundance, and integrity! And so it is!" These are words that I was inspired to write. I am forgiveness, I am unconditional love, and I am peace. I knew I must forgive myself first, and then forgive everyone and everything, in order for me to move forward in a positive way. My CD player in the car and at home was constantly playing some kind of motivational music or lecture. It was so empowering, and I was feeling great! I felt happy and at peace.

I am so grateful for the opportunity that I had to experience single life in the later stage of my life. I actually embraced it. I learned that we are never too old to set another goal or to dream another dream. To continually reinvent your self is the key to remaining youthful.

CHAPTER 22

After my divorce, it was important to me that I was focused on Trenton, I wanted to be there for him always. He had a room at my house and spent a lot of time with me. I loved the nights that he and his friends would come home after a social night out, sit on my bed, and tell me all the stories of that night. It was a very special time. I had made the commitment to myself not to do any serious dating while Trenton was preparing to go on a service mission for the LDS church. The Church of Jesus Christ of Latter Day Saints has a missionary program for the youth. If they choose to do so, they are sent worldwide for up to two years to preach the gospel and serve their fellowman. After he left on his two-year mission to the state of Alaska, I started to date more. My girlfriend had to convince me to set myself up on my first internet dating site, (which I said I would never do.) I eventually was on four different Internet sites. It kept me from being lonesome at night, and I made friends from all over. I felt it was safe; I was in the safety of my own home, I would talk with them online for a while, and then the relationships progressed to the telephone. I met a few of them in person, and I always took precautions. I made some great friends! I also went to church dances. I'll never forget my first church dance. I was so nervous that I sat in my car for half an hour before I got the courage to finally walk in by myself. I made some awesome friends and had a blast dancing.

Great exercise! I tried to be nice to everyone. People are lonesome and just looking for places to socialize and have friends.

I had so many girlfriends that were negative about men. Because of their past experiences, they had developed some fixed beliefs about men in general. Some of those were: "All men want is a nurse and a purse," "All men want is sex, money, power," and "All men are alike: men are jerks!" Relationships are a risk, but I refused to believe all men were jerks. I knew that there were some great men out there and kept believing that there was a perfect relationship for me somewhere, sometime. I realized that what you believe, you attract! I also noticed how we can have such high expectations, and because of them we are continually disappointed.

My whole philosophy was fun and friends. I had been married for thirty years and had my family. I didn't worry about getting married again; I was perfectly happy and content with my life. I was empowered to create my life going forward. I do love companionship, and I knew what I wanted and deserved now. I wasn't going to settle for anything less. I wrote down my affirmations: "I am attracting love and peace into my life. I am attracting the perfect relationship for me." I made the list of qualities I wanted in a man and had it on my bedside table. Those qualities were integrity, a good heart, a sense of humor, communication, healthy and active, self-motivated, spiritual, abundant, open-minded, and he treats me like a queen! I knew that in order to attract my perfect relationship, I deserved to be those things also. It would serve me to believe that there was a perfect man for me. I wrote down that I was attracting the perfect relationship for me at the perfect time. I thought it, I believed it, I visualized it, I felt it, I wrote it, and I released it with gratitude. Then I got out, met people, and was active in my life.

I was inspired to create a singles networking group. I saw how people just craved for a place to get together and socialize. I didn't want a dating service, there are plenty of those. I wanted a support group, a group of singles that enjoyed being friends and supported one another in various ways. I had a diverse group of friends, because I was out in the community so much. I had single friends all over the place. I invited about fifty people to my home for the kick-off event. It was to be a potluck social. I have to admit, I had several negative responses from a couple of the ladies. They said," Oh, you'll never get any guys to attend something like that!" Well, guess what? I had twenty-five attend that first night, and over 50 percent were men! It was a talented, enthusiastic, and successful group of singles. We ate, played games, laughed, and socialized until one thirty in the morning. It was great! I explained to them what I had a clear intention of creating, and they all were excited to be a part of it. I moved forward with getting an e-mail list and providing an event a month. We did so many things: art festivals, plays, hikes, cookouts, and movies with pizza. If anyone in our group had anything that they wanted participants or support for, I would send out a mass e-mail letting everyone know. Those that could show up would come. I really enjoyed the association of the people of Connections, and it was fulfilling a need for social experiences with great people.

In 2009 I had been divorced for two and a half years. I had sent my son on his mission to Alaska, had been super-busy with my work, and had been traveling a lot performing my Celine act. Life was great, and God had blessed me to stay busy so that I wouldn't grieve too much over Trent being gone. I didn't see him for two years and spoke with him only on Mother's Day and Christmas. It was something he really wanted to do, and I supported him in that. It was important for him to start his own journey.

SECTION 4

A HAWAIIAN ROMANCE

CHAPTER 23

Seek out that particular mental attribute which makes you feel most deeply and vitally alive, along with which comes the inner voice which says, 'this is the real me,' and when you have found that attitude, follow it.

—*William James*

I set my book aside and looked out over the deep Pacific Ocean. I reminisced back to June 2007, when I was flying to Hawaii with my girlfriend Kim for our girlfriend's getaway. I wouldn't be on this trip to Bali, without a fateful trip to Hawaii first. The idea of going to Hawaii all started with my friend Selma Kull, from Washington. She came to Green Valley, the destination spa where I worked, every year for twenty years, at least as long as I had been there. She was a sweetheart, and everyone looked forward to seeing her when she came back. She attended all the fitness classes and made all the hikes. She was over seventy and was living life to the fullest. She was an inspiration to everyone who knew her. Every year Selma said to me, "Why don't you go to Hawaii and use my condo in Waikiki for a week?" The timing had never been right for me, not until then. I thought about it seriously for the first time, but with whom would I go? One Sunday my girlfriend Kim was over to work on an event for Connections, the singles networking group that I started, and on impulse I asked her, "Hey, do you want to go to Hawaii with me?" She looked at me and without too much hesitation said, "Sure!"

We were both looking forward to the experience, and both of us were full of enthusiasm and anticipation for what was to come next in our lives. I told Kim that this would be a trip of a lifetime and that I was sure we would meet some great people and have a blast! In conversation I also told her we would meet some cute guys that would show us around and treat us to dinner. She laughed and responded, "Ok" with a big smile. I had been to Hawaii in the eighties but didn't remember much, other than that I missed my babies. This was a spontaneous girlfriend's getaway to celebrate my fifty-fifth birthday. Within two hours, with no specific itinerary or plan in mind except to have fun, we had booked our flight. Two weeks later we were on a flight from Las Vegas to Honolulu for a week of incredible fun, adventure, and lifetime memories. We met new people everywhere we went, who quickly became our friends. They offered advice and assistance that opened new doors of opportunity and adventure for us to explore while we were in Hawaii. Little did we know what was in store for us! Every day we walked a short distance from my friend's condo to the Hilton Hawaiian Village Resort. We enjoyed their first-class facilities, man-made lagoon, tropical gardens and wildlife, boutique shops, and ocean view restaurants. Our daily treat was a scoop of Lappert's Hawaiian macadamia nut ice cream!

Right away we began to plan our week. We stopped at a kiosk and agreed to go to a presentation for Travel Destinations, so that we could get great discounts on our activities. We committed to each other that we weren't going to buy any real estate or time shares, but Kim ended up buying into the program. She put me on the contract, because we had big plans of traveling the world together in the future. We made friends with the marketing executives, and after the presentation we went with them to a place called The Shack. It was a popular place for drinks and dancing. It was a fun night. I don't drink, but I love to dance!

Friday, June 12, 2009, was the day that changed my life forever! Our friend Jeff, from the Travel Destinations group, called and invited us to meet them at a high-class night club, Rumors, at the Ala Moana Hotel. It was walking distance from our condo, so we agreed to meet them.

Kim and I arrived at the nightclub and were looking for our friends for about ten minutes, when in walked the most handsome man! Now, Rumors was full of good-looking men, but this one stood out to me! He was in jeans and an orange-rust-colored aloha shirt. He had the athletic look; he resembled a football player. He was about six foot, with dark hair that was slightly grey on the sides. He had beautiful blue eyes and dimples, and a smile that swept me away. When our eyes met, there was a connection. I looked away, not wanting to be too obvious. Kim and I found our friends and sat at a table up on a tier along the dance floor. The music was great, and there was a lot of dancing. I kept my eye on this handsome man, who was with a younger man. Kim came over to me and pointed them out, saying that they kept looking at us. I laughed and said, "Really?" But I knew he was watching me too. I could feel it!

It was so much fun to be there with the people and the music. Dancing is therapeutic in so many ways. As I was on the dance floor with Jeff, I could see my "dream man" standing at the other side of the dance floor. He and the other young man walked over to our table. They asked my friend Kim and another girl to dance. Kim accepted and ended up on the dance floor with the younger man, whose name was Eric. When the song was over, I had my eye on "my" man, who was standing at the other end of the dance floor. Without hesitation I walked over to him and asked him to dance. He looked surprised but set his drink down, and we danced. He was a great dancer! That really impressed me.

It turned out that Eric was the son of this beautiful man, Mark Charles Mahler. I invited them both to join our group. I liked Mark right off! Divorced for three years and through the process of dating again, he told me that he realized he was a great catch: "I have all my teeth, I have a job, a car, and I don't live with my parents." Hey, he had a sense of humor too! We sat and talked, getting to know each other. We laughed, danced, and had a blast! I was in for a Hawaiian romance.

I had established a personal standard "no kissing on the first date." I had lived up to that with my dating experiences so far. That didn't work so well when I met Mark. We walked outside to the patio, where we intended to cool off and take in the evening breeze. It was a beautiful Hawaiian night. He sat in front of me holding my hands, and I stood looking down into his beautiful blue eyes. He pulled me to him and kissed me! I felt all bubbly inside, like a bottle of 7 up when you take off the top! Then I said, "That was our first kiss." Mark told me later that, by my comment, he knew there would be more kisses.

Mark leaned forward on the table toward me and looked at me as if he were analyzing me. As he talked, he appeared confident. Instead of scaring me, he drew me in. I loved his confidence. He told me that he could tell that I was just being who I am, not trying to be what I thought he wanted. That phrase in particular really hit me. It was so true. From the start, I felt comfortable being who I was and being true to myself. This would lead to be the foundation of our relationship and Mark would often say that he fell in love with me just being me.

Kim and I decided to let Mark and Eric give us a tour of the island, since they offered. We made arrangements for them to pick us up the following day. Mark said he would call around four. The next day, two minutes before four, Mark called. He was true to his word.

I have to say that when I saw Mark, it was like opening that bottle of 7 Up again. It wasn't a nervous feeling, because I felt so at ease with him and could be myself. I kept asking myself, *Is this what it feels like? Love at first sight?* It was different than anything I had experienced. I believed in love at first sight, in a match made in heaven, and I also believed there are certain choices that lead to attracting a soul mate. Was I finally experiencing it?

We had a wonderful day! The four of us toured the island. We talked and laughed all the way up the coast. We went up the east side, past Diamond Head Crater, Hanauma Bay, and the Blow Hole. It was a beautiful ride on the coast heading north. We drove over Interstate H-3 and went west to Ko'Olina Resort. We had Hawaiian drinks at Long Boards Grill, at the Marriott Beach Club, and then walked the lagoons to see the sunset.

When the sun is going down on the horizon and the conditions are just perfect, that very last spark of light can be a "green flash." Some people say it isn't real, because they have never seen it, but Mark and I saw it that night. We said it was just another sign that it was meant for us to meet. We went to dinner after the sunset at Roy's, a very nice restaurant on the golf course in Ko'Olina. What a romantic evening it was. Mark knew just how to treat a lady.

131

Mark and Eric had planned to go skydiving the next day and asked us if we wanted to join them. My first response was to say that I would go but not skydive. Kim didn't let me get away with that one! It was my fifty-fifth birthday, and she thought I really deserved to experience skydiving over Hawaii. After much convincing, I agreed that I would give it a try. Mark and Eric picked us up the next morning, and off we went to Dillingham Airfield on the northwest side of the island. I was feeling pretty empowered after all my courses with Impact Training. In one of the programs they called "LIFTOFF," we did a rope course that was quite challenging. It gave us the opportunity to face our fears and overcome them. I'm sure that experience assisted me in having the courage to try skydiving. We had to sign a release form that was about ten pages, and on the bottom of each page in big black bold letters it said, "Warning! This activity can cause bodily injury or DEATH!" Oh great! I had to just cover that with my hand and sign.

I could try to describe how it feels skydiving, but until you actually experience it, no one can even imagine what it is like! I'm sure everyone's adventure is unique. We had to wait all day for our turn. When it was time, we were ready, willing, and waiting. Each of us was buckled into a harness to experience tandem skydiving with a licensed instructor. As the plane soared to fifteen thousand feet, I admit, I wondered a little bit what I was doing! I said to myself over and over, "I am protected! I am protected! I am protected!" There were four of us, eight with our instructors. Talk about faith in whomever you were attached to! I figured he didn't want to die that day either, so that comforted me a little … just a little!

Eric went out first, then Mark, Kim, and, yes, I was the last to jump. At that point there was no turning back. I closed my eyes, and out we went. I couldn't breathe. I just couldn't catch my breath. We were falling at 120 miles per hour! I finally opened my eyes, one eye at a time. Just to peek. My instructor pulled the cord to open the chute. Yay, it opened! I started to relax and felt much better. It was beautiful flying high above the Oahu coast! Then my instructor said, "Oh, it looks like one of your friends' parachutes did not open!" *What?* I learned that Eric's primary chute had not opened, so they had to use the secondary chute. He got an extra freefall! All I could think about was how grateful I was that it hadn't been me, because I really didn't want an extra freefall. Eric thought that the experience was way cool. It certainly created something to talk about later. My landing was a breeze. I just lifted my feet up, and the instructor took us in. I did it! I made it! I had created another awesome memory. I'm so glad I worked through my fear to try it. I could now mark that off my bucket list.

We had gotten our adrenaline rush for the day, so we headed to Mililani for a barbecue at Mark's house. It was a beautiful home. I met his dog, Shelby, a fourteen-year-old golden retriever. I learned at the time that Eric had just moved from Denver a few months earlier, to live with Mark. That's where Mark had lived for twenty-five years. He was born in Tacoma, Washington and grew up in Woodland Hills, California. Mark had planned my favorite meal, salmon on the grill. After dinner we played games for hours, Guesstures, Pictionary, etc. I had found a guy that actually would play games and have fun with it—how cool is that? I had to chalk up another plus in his favor. That night Mark asked me to go to dinner the next evening, just the two of us. It would be our first date without Kim and Eric, who had been great sports!

Mark picked me up after he finished work around five in the evening. We went to the Sheraton Hotel in Waikiki and sat on the patio to watch the sunset and have a drink. It was a perfect evening. We sat and talked for the longest time, then took our shoes off and walked the beach, caught up in each other and the great conversation. The more I learned about Mark, the more fascinated I was. I knew I had never met anyone like him before. After drinks and a sunset walk, we had a nice dinner at a restaurant right on the water, Blue Water Grill. Afterward, we drove to a secluded beach in Kailua, Lanikai. The sky was clear and the stars bright. We found a place on the beach, sat and talked and looked at the stars. I was leaving in the morning, and this would be the last evening spent with this amazing man. I really felt he was special, and knowing him just for these few days convinced me that he was perfect for me. I honestly could not find anything about him I wanted to change. It was a relationship that I would love to pursue, but I lived three thousand miles way!

CHAPTER 24

Mark brought me back to the condo that same night around one in the morning. Kim was in bed and had packed for our departure early the next morning. We had made arrangements to take a shuttle to the airport. We had to be at the airport by five thirty in the morning. Mark insisted that we cancel the shuttle, saying he would make sure we got there. He went home to Mililani and came back by five o'clock to pick us up. He loaded our luggage, drove us to the airport, unloaded our luggage, and made sure we got through the security check. He told me that we would see each other again. I saw him standing against the wall, watching us as we passed through security. I felt he was looking at me with loving eyes. I knew I would see him again; I just didn't know when. As Kim and I were making our way to the gate, I received a text from Mark that said, "You are an unbelievable gift. A gift I believe in!" I thought, *How great is that?* I responded, "I believe in us!" We boarded the airplane—and up, up, and away!

Kim and I talked about our wonderful girl's getaway in Hawaii and what we had learned. Kim said, "Life is short, so talk to strangers and make new friends every day. Be bold enough to walk through open doors of opportunity ... you never know who you'll meet and what adventures are just around the corner. I loved my first girlfriend's getaway!"

135

I said, "We own all power and authority over our lives and control our destiny. So live life to the fullest and with courage—watch what happens! Then take a leap of faith, literally, and do things that really push you out of your comfort zone!" Our time in Hawaii was truly magical. The highlight for me was meeting Mark. I knew I wanted to see him again, that he had stolen my heart. When we landed in Las Vegas, I had a text message from him on my phone: "Believing in each other is a great place to start, and we started off great!" And there was a picture of a rose. How romantic is that?

It always takes a few days to get back into reality after a vacation, especially this vacation. I kept thinking it was a dream. Mark and I talked on the phone and texted throughout the day. Mark's texts always made me smile. However, I was caught off guard by one of them.

> Wednesday, June 17, 2009
>
> 10:26 a.m. "My day started off great! I thought of how blessed I am to have met you"
>
> 1:08 p.m. "You just brought a huge smile to my face! Xoxoxoxo☺"
>
> 3:54 p.m. "Hi babe, ... Would it be better for you to pick me up in St. George this Friday at 5:00 p.m. or 11:30 p.m.?"

What? Did he mean he was coming to Utah to see me? I'd been home only two days! Wow! I called Mark right away. Sure enough, he planned to visit me this weekend. I told him I would pick him up at five in the evening, and I made arrangements for him to stay at Green Valley Resort, where I worked. I was quite impressed with his efforts to be with me. Just one more thing to love about him! How neat to have someone think that I was worth the time and money to travel over three thousand miles for one weekend!

After receiving the following texts from Mark, I realized how special our relationship was, even at this new beginning. I was so looking forward to seeing him.

Thursday, June 18, 2009

9:32 a.m. "Good morning, Sunshine! I am smiling so much my face hurts."

3:20 p.m. "It's so nice to feel this way again … surreal … a wonderful place to be. I enjoy every moment, feel it in my heart, and smile so the rest of the world can see!☺"

As I thought about the events of the last week, I reflected on some things that had happened prior to meeting Mark. Over the past few years, I had been open to certain readings done by spiritual counselors. One was a dear friend, and the others were acquaintances who were referred me by close friends. I couldn't help but reflect on how all of them had said that the perfect man would come into my life, that he would be my dream man, a man too great to be true. I wouldn't think that he could possibly be for real, but I should open my heart and eliminate all fear because it would be the real thing. I felt this was the man they were talking about … I truly did!

I have to admit this was moving fast enough to make my head spin, and there was that element of fear creeping in now and then.

It's natural to close off our hearts due to past experiences. No one wants to have a broken heart, but it's better to have had than not to have had at all! It was the advice to stay open to the possibility that this was for real that kept me anxious to move forward. I was thankful for that insight. I was thankful for the faith to know that this man came into my life for a reason. I was going to go for it!

Friday, June 19, five o'clock couldn't have come any faster. I left work to pick Mark up from the airport. He flew right into St. George, Utah, so it was easy. He was waiting for me with that big smile, those dimples, and those beautiful blue eyes. I felt those bubbles again! We embraced passionately. It sure was easy to kiss this man. We went to my house, so I could change for a hike and dinner. I grabbed a swimsuit, and off we went. We had fun hiking to the petroglyphs out in Ivins. Afterward, I introduced him to the Mexican restaurant Café Rio, in St. George. We took the burritos back to Green Valley, sat on the lanai, and enjoyed our dinner together. It was great to be together again. After dinner we went swimming and sat in the hot tub. It was a beautiful night in southern Utah. He was in my territory now. How cool that he was here!

The next morning, I picked him up and we went to Zion National Park for a hike. We had lunch at Oscar's, a Mexican grill with a view of the Zion Mountains. I knew that terrain well and enjoyed sharing the spectacular view with him. We continued to enjoy the day.

I had an event with my singles networking group that night, so Mark came along. I told him that we couldn't attend as a couple, because it was a group of single friends. We went to the barbecue and production of *Footloose* at Tuacahn outdoor theater. I had several friends in the play; it was fun to support them. It wasn't that easy to act like we weren't in "in like" status. My friends picked up on it right away. We all enjoyed the evening, and it was fun to see Mark interact with my friends. He fit in right away, and they all liked him very much.

On Sunday, Mark came with me to the fitness classes I taught. No one came to my water fitness class, so we were able to sit by the pool and visit. He told me he already knew that he loved me. I said that I had feelings for him also but suggested we give it six months and see where it went. I knew that he was special.

On Father's Day I arranged a special dinner with my special friends Cindy and Del Pulsipher. Cindy was my best friend, so I really wanted her to meet Mark. She had spoken to Mark on the phone and asked him if he was "the real thing." I laughed because I think everyone thought that. We went to dinner at the restaurant Cosmopolitan in Silver Reef. We had a great time. Del and Cindy loved Mark. I knew they would. He treated me with such love and respect, I had to pinch myself! I did deserve it and I loved every minute of it.

Mark flew out Monday morning. We had a beautiful weekend and knew that we wanted to pursue a relationship, even though it would be long-distance. The texting and phone calls from Mark began again. Long distance dating had gotten easier with all the new technology.

> June 22, 2009 6:48 a.m. "Ours is an amazing romance. I'm on the plane flying in the wrong direction! Xoxo"

> June 23, 2009 11:15 a.m. "I love you. Woke up this morning thinking of you"

June 26, 2009 1:39 p.m. "Thinking of you brings a smile to my face☺"

June 27, 2009 9:06 a.m. "God has blessed both of us … as a result my heart is filled with JOY and HAPPINESS!"

CHAPTER 25

The greatest challenge of the human experience
is discovering who you are. The second greatest is
living in a way that honors what you discovered.
—Impact Trainings

Mark and I both felt comfortable being just who we are, and
I think that is so important for those men and women who
are looking for a valid relationship. So many times we want to
change for someone, thinking it will make them love us more; and
sometimes we want to change them. It is exhausting to try to be
something you are not. If you can't be the real you, then you are
with the wrong person. Be completely who you are, and you will
attract the right person.

One of the most special things about our relationship was that
we were in a similar place of spiritual belief. I had been raised
Mormon, and Mark was raised Catholic. Both of us had received
great religious foundations and had been open to a new level of
discovering our own spirituality. We had many discussions about
"laws of the universe." I shared with him the book *The Secret*,
about the law of attraction, which I believe in and have used. We
both agreed that we were on the same energy frequency to have
met and connected the way that we did. Coming into each other's

lives was inevitable. We spent many hours on the phone, over four thousand minutes in one month on our cell phones!

The next time Mark came to see me, he asked me to learn to scuba dive. This was one of his passions. I knew that this would be a hard thing for me to do. Since I had lost my sons, I had not been able to put my head in the water without having an anxiety attack. It actually surprised me when I experienced overwhelming fear for the first time while snorkeling in Cancun, Mexico. I did not know that my experience with my sons had left such an impression in my sub-conscious mind, but I did know that I did not want to live in fear and miss out on life! I decided that I would do my best to overcome this anxiety which came from my past experience. We rented equipment from the dive shop in St. George and headed for the Green Valley pool. Mark was patient as I tried to get used to putting my head under the water and breathing through the regulator. It was a weird feeling for me and somewhat claustrophobic. I had to fight anxiety attacks. I wasn't going to give up. The way that I was able to overcome the fear was to focus on my breathing as if I was in a yoga class. Mark said if I wanted lessons to learn how to dive, he would pay for them. I began studying and preparing to get certified in scuba diving. The book work wasn't too hard, and I passed all the written tests, but I had a hard time passing the underwater skills. I deserved to experience diving now that Mark had brought this opportunity into my life. This was an opportunity to develop courage again and overcome a barrier.

My first open-water dive was a disaster! My instructor took me to Quail Creek reservoir on a hot summer day, about 108 degrees. We dressed in our wetsuits, booties, tanks, BCD vests, flippers, etc. and hiked down a rocky hill to the dive site. It was muddy, and we would sink into the mud with every step. I was hot and worn out before I even started the dive. Though the water was real murky and muddy, it felt great, because we were so overheated. We were supposed to go down a line to the bottom of the lake. I went down about ten feet and panicked; I had to come up. It was so murky I could not see a thing. I was disappointed that I didn't complete my open-water dive.

Mark had me wait until my trip to Hawaii in November to finish. He said it would be much easier in the ocean because of the clear water, and there would be lots to see. I did end up completing my scuba certification in Hawaii. I did it! Yay! I had to learn to talk myself through it and not allow fear to set in. I learned to focus and really control my thoughts. My motivation to overcome my fear was not only for me, but for my son Trent. I didn't want him to live his life in fear because of what happened to his brothers. He deserved to live life fearlessly. I wanted to be an example of courage to him. Being a parent is living as an example to your children for the things that you want to teach them. That was my biggest motivation.

Through the summer, Mark flew over to see me when he could, usually about every two weeks. His phone calls and the texting were nonstop.

> July 9, 2009, 9:00 a.m. "You are the most beautiful woman I have ever known!"

> July 16, 2009 12:15 p.m. "There is no greater gift you can give me than your heart … which is exactly why I give you mine … without reservation without condition."

> July 20, 2009 3:52 p.m. "You are perfect for me … loving you is so easy!"

Thirty days passed before we saw each other again. I missed Mark so much, and time went so slowly when we weren't together. He was so romantic even from so far away. I would receive beautiful flowers regularly, with wonderful notes of affection. We started talking about marriage very early in the relationship. He wanted to know how I felt about it. Before I met Mark, I really didn't know if I want to get married again. I had my family, could take care of myself, and was content and happy in my life. But when he asked me if I would consider marriage, I really didn't think twice. I knew I wanted to be with him, and I wouldn't give up my life in Utah without being married. I am traditional and believe in the institution of marriage, especially when you feel it is so right.

One weekend when Mark flew in, we went to Marysvale, Utah, and stayed at the Old Pine Hotel. It was a bed-and-breakfast resort and had become one of my favorite places in recent years. I wanted to share it with Mark. We got ATVs and drove over Cottonwood Loop, hiked to a cool waterfall, and toured Miners' Park. We covered those mountains! We went to Bryce Canyon and hiked Sunrise Point, having a great time together. We both love the mountains. It was at the top of Sunrise Point that Mark asked me to marry him. I had no problem saying, *"Yes, yes, yes!"* He said that he would make it official when I came to Hawaii in a few weeks.

Mark asked me if I wanted to assist him in picking out my ring, or if it was okay to surprise me and do it himself. I was open to the latter; I knew he had good taste, and I knew it would be nice.

CHAPTER 26

Mark arranged for me to fly to Hawaii on September 3, 2009. Upon landing in Honolulu the anticipation of seeing Mark grew. I was so excited to be with him! He met me at the gate, holding a sign that read, *"HH (Hawaiian Hunk) Ocean Tours Bonnie Luke, where Hawaiian Romance lasts a lifetime."* We were off to Kauai for the weekend. This was a big weekend, because I just knew that he was going to officially propose to me and give me a ring! He had rented a red convertible, and we stayed at a place right on the ocean, Whalers Cove. It was fabulous! I was living a dream, in paradise with the man of my dreams, the love of my life!

After settling in, Mark gave me the first hand-written clue to a scavenger hunt he had created. It said, "I knew from the moment I saw you that I wanted to meet you ... To read more you deserve a warm snack ... go to the microwave."

Clue #2 "After I met you I wanted to get to know you ... To read more you deserve a cold drink ... go to the refrigerator"

Clue #3 "As I learned more about you I wanted to kiss you ... to read more you deserve some ice for your drink ... go to the freezer"

Clue #4 "The chemistry I felt when I kissed you told me I wanted to spend more time with you … to read more you deserve a scenic rest … go to the lanai."

Clue #5 "The more time I spent with you the more I loved you … to read more you deserve to go to the restroom"

Clue #6 "The more I loved you, the more I wanted to share the rest of my life with you … to read more you deserve to go to the bedroom."

When I entered the bedroom, on the bed was another clue.

Clue #7 said, "You truly are the love of my life and the woman of my dreams! I Love, Adore, Cherish, Respect, Honor, Appreciate, Recognize, Admire, and Trust you! I am Passionate & Crazy about You!" "WILL YOU" …

And as I finished reading, there was Mark on his knees with the ring box in his hands. He said, *"Marry me?."* … and opened the box to present a most unique and beautiful solitaire, a Montana Yogo sapphire with half-carat diamonds on the side, set in platinum. The color was an amazing cornflower blue. *I loved it!* I knew he would pick out something awesome, and I was right. These stones are mined only in Montana and are very rare. His mother has one too, and that makes it extra special.

Mark is so generous, and I know he loves me very much. I never would have imagined such a love. We really are perfect for each other! It was definitely a romantic evening: sunset dinner at Roy's right on the ocean, and a long walk on the beach. All I can say is that the spiritual, emotional, and physical connection we have is amazing. I love this man with all my heart.

The rest of the weekend included zip-lining in the mountains of Kauai, hiking to Waimea Falls, and sunset dinners. We flew back to Oahu on Sunday night and went to what was going to be my new home as Mrs. Mark Charles Mahler, Ko'Olina Resort, on the west side of Oahu. It is so beautiful, and I am really close to the ocean, only a five- or ten-minute walk. On Monday we went scuba diving at Sharks Cove with Mark's best friends Stu and Rita. Quality people! The next morning I headed home to Utah, as an officially engaged woman, with my beautiful ring on my finger. I have to admit it was hard to leave. Mark would be coming to Utah in a few weeks, but that would be an eternity to me.

Time passed, as it always does. Mark came out to Utah later that October to meet my family. We went to Logan for the weekend. My family welcomed him with open arms and gave us an engagement party. My sister Kathy and her husband, Gary, took us four-wheeling up the canyon. Mark fit in with my family so well. That meant a lot to me.

It was getting closer to our wedding date of December 27. It was so hard to be without each other through those last couple of months. I planned to go to Hawaii for Thanksgiving, then come back home to quit my jobs and start packing to move. What happened was that I quit my jobs early and stayed in Hawaii for three weeks. Mark paid my bills for the month of December, so for the first time in my life I didn't have a job. I was okay with it for the moment.

When I met Mark, I knew he had a great job, but I really didn't pay much attention to that. I just knew he treated me like a queen and put forth the effort to do what it took to be with me. Certain thoughts did enter my mind: *Am I caught up in all this romance? Is this for real? I have a man that makes a great living and wants to take care of me?* He knew I would be giving up a lot to marry him and move to Hawaii, so he told me I could go home whenever I wanted to. I have to admit that made it a little easier, knowing that I would be able to see my family with his complete support.

Now, this is the trick that life plays! A few days after I arrived for the Thanksgiving holiday, Mark came home from work and said that the company he worked for eliminated his position, he had been laid off. We had the option of taking a severance package or a similar position with a cut in pay and a transfer to Buffalo, New York. We talked about it and decided to take the severance and stay in Hawaii. Here we were, with no jobs and getting married the next month. Faith was the name of the game at this stage. It was an adventure, and we were going to work it out.

I knew everything would work out fine. Not once did I doubt my decision to marry Mark or what we were planning for our future together. I got a job right away with the Marriott Wellness Center, teaching White Tiger Yoga on the beach. Perfect! I settled in Hawaii, and they agreed to let me start in February or March. God blessed me once again! Mark continued to job hunt.

I flew home to start preparing for a new adventure in my life, my marriage to the man of my dreams, never once doubting my decision. It was a huge job packing up my house in St. George. Decisions of what to leave and what to take—I didn't have a clue! I had filled a three-bedroom home with furniture and other belongings. I knew that I could not take it all to Hawaii. I finally made decisions about what was important to me and began packing it up. I continued to plan the wedding, with Mark in Hawaii and myself in St. George. We planned to be married on December 27, in Montana at the Mahler lake house on Whitefish Lake, which lies at the base of Glacier National Park. We were planning on spending Christmas that year with Mark's family anyway and thought it would be easier for everyone to come there for the wedding than to fly all the way to Hawaii. So it would be a winter-white wedding. I invited all my family, but Melody wasn't in the position to commit, and Mom's health wasn't good. We flew Kathy up for the wedding; she will never know how much it meant to me to be able to share it with someone in my family! Trenton was still on his service mission in Alaska, so he was not able to be there. I really missed him but knew that he understood.

The wedding was a black/white wedding, with the men in black suits, the women in black dresses. I wore a beautiful white suit with a white fur collar that I special ordered. It was perfect for my winter wedding in Montana. Mark's father married us, which was so very special for us and for him. In Montana anybody can marry you. Mark's children, Stephanie and Eric, came from Denver for the wedding after being with their mother for Christmas. My sweet mother-in-law, Joanne, provided the flowers and the food. Everything was perfect! The ground was covered with lots of white, driven snow and the lake was frozen solid. The beauty was magical. This was truly a dream!

Mark and I used the book *The Four Agreements* as the foundation of our vows: (1) be impeccable with your word; (2) don't take anything personally; (3) don't make assumptions; and (4) do the best you can! He was open to applying these principles in his life; that was another sign to me that he was the perfect man for me. These principles are some of the things that I strive to live by in my own life. How cool, to find someone who will support me in these things!

January 2010, I started a whole new adventure in my life. Not in my wildest imagination did I ever think that I would one day live in beautiful Hawaii, the most isolated place in the whole world. I was with the love of my life, and together we had the opportunity to create a whole new future. From the first day I was here, I woke up to cool trade wind breezes, palm trees outside my window, and mynah birds singing. I felt like I was in a dream. What a paradise! I embraced each day with enthusiasm for a new adventure. I wanted to create a heaven on earth in our home. Hawaii was the perfect place for a life of peace. Our home is where the heart is, a place of refuge from the chaos and drama of the world. I would do my part to create a place for Mark to come home to and feel loved, appreciated, and recognized.

Mark and I spent a few months in Hawaii before we left for our honeymoon in Palau; we were planning to stay on a live-aboard scuba dive boat called the *Aggressor*. Mark had previously planned this trip about one year ago. It was before he had met me, and we both decided that it would make the perfect honeymoon. The *Aggressor* traveled through the Rock Islands for seven days. We would be going with Mark's dear friends Stu and Rita Ganz. Palau is one of the top ten places in the world to dive. It is in the Mariana Islands south of Guam. They say that if God were a scuba diver, he would dive in Palau!

CHAPTER 27

Palau is such a beautiful place. The water is crystal clear blue, and the beaches are covered with fine white sand. I couldn't believe where I was! Everyone on board was an experienced diver, and I was new to it all. It was a small, intimate group, and we became close friends. We ate, slept, and dived every day for seven days. I did about two dives a day, and most everyone else did four or five dives a day.

My first dive was a shipwreck at a depth of about seventy feet. The water wasn't very clear, and I stressed a little. Putting mind over body had to kick in. Scuba diving was a lot of work for me. It was not only mentally challenging but physically exhausting, from fighting the currents. I worked hard at trying to focus and relax! I do specifically remember a couple of dives that were amazing. Most of our dives were between fifty and sixty feet deep. Some of the other dives were much deeper, so I did not dive them at the time. One wall dive was supposed to be at fifty feet. I had been having a difficult time sinking so Mark intentionally over weighted me. I sank like a rock! Mark was right there with me trying to stabilize me, and I noticed the other divers were quite a bit above us. I looked at my depth gage and saw that we were at eighty feet! I looked at Mark and gave him my best "stink eye" look. By that time I had enough air in my BCD and we rose up to finish the dive with the rest of the group. When we got back on the boat I asked Mark how we got to eighty feet? He said with a big grin, "We came up twenty feet!" It was then that I learned I had done my first one hundred foot dive. Another signature dive, Blue Corners, was incredible. I descended last, with an instructor assigned to me because I was a new diver. The current was strong, and he had to hold on to me, or I would've been swept to China! I'll never forget the colors as we dropped into an awesome canyon of the world underwater. It was amazing. We all had reef hooks that we hooked into our BCDs and then into the reef. We could float with the current and watch the life underwater go by. We saw all sizes and kinds of colorful fish and sharks. It felt like I was flying underwater. All my senses came alive in this awesome experience.

As we cruised around the Rock Islands, I took in all the wonder of a completely different world! On one of the islands there was a natural phenomenon called Jellyfish Lake. This body of water had originally been part of the ocean. It remained a saltwater lake and home to thousands of jellyfish that had evolved without stingers because there were no predators. We took a boat to the island early in the morning, as the sun was just coming up. We hiked through the jungle, and when we reached the lake, we could see the sun shining on the other side. The jellyfish follow the sun, so we jumped in and snorkeled toward the sunny part of the lake. As we swam the jellyfish began to appear, at first twenty or thirty, then a couple hundred, then thousands. We were actually swimming right into a sea of jellyfish! Large ones, medium-sized ones, babies riding on their mamas. They were everywhere, and we could hardly believe our eyes. It was truly one of the highlights of the trip. And we continued to sleep, eat, dive, and sleep, eat, dive!

After returning home, I started doing personal training and teaching yoga and Pilates for the Marriott Wellness Center in Ko'Olina. I could walk to work in ten minutes. I also managed an ice cream parlor called "Two Scoops" in the evenings, while we built our scuba diving company, Captain Bruce. Mark wanted the experience of owning his own business, and because he loved diving we bought an existing scuba company. We invested our retirement funds in it and totally revamped the company. We knew it was a risk, but Mark deserved the opportunity to have his own business if that is what he wanted. We fixed the boat up to be the most beautiful on the island. We bought a Mercedes sprinter van with a limo conversion inside; we had a hot shower, warm towels, and catered food. Our staff was trained to provide quality customer service. We really raised the bar for a quality dive experience on this island.

After going on a live-a-board in Palau for our honeymoon, and seeing how wonderful the customer service was, we wanted to create that on our boat. We brainstormed for hours as we walked the Ko'Olina lagoons every night, coming up with ideas and putting together plans of how to create great memories for our dive clients. During our first year of marriage, we were together constantly, building Captain Bruce Scuba Tours. It was 24-7 working the business, but we enjoyed being together. We worked hard and the business went everywhere we went! Until you have had a business of your own and experienced the blood, sweat, and tears of it, you cannot even realize the effort that goes into making it successful. We provided jobs for fifteen employees, and until they and our overhead had been paid, we didn't get paid. After about six months we realized that we couldn't make the living that we wanted with this business, and Mark resumed his job search. By the end of the year Mark was working for Kaiser

Permanente and the following May we sold our scuba company. Captain Bruce Scuba Tours taught us both a lot. I learned much about diving that I never knew! I loved going out on the boat and associating with our staff, friends, and clients. I had every bit of confidence in Mark, because of the person he is, and admired his hard work and integrity. We both say to this very day what a great experience it was, and we are thankful for it!

Mark and I have a townhome in Ko'Olina Resort. I love it. The area is secured and the landscape is beautifully maintained. We've met a lot of great people. I love Hawaii, the culture, the diversity in race, religion, personalities, body types, and lifestyles. My work at the Marriott Wellness Center is a blessing! I meet people from all over the world; visiting and working with these people adds so much to my life. It expands my understanding of mankind. It is a perfect place to learn acceptance of all God's children and the unique qualities that each of us brings to this world. I feel like I have it all. The secret to having it all, is believing that you already do. I do believe! It is a dream life with my dream man.

To be with Mark and adjusting to my new life in Hawaii did take time and patience on my part. I chose to leave my life in St. George and everything that I had built for thirty years. It definitely was a little scary, but I never have had any regrets. Life is full of adjustments, change, and new opportunities, and I certainly had experienced plenty of that! Mark was the love of my life, and I knew that I wanted to be with him.

Arthur Rubenstein said, *"I have found that if you love life, life will love you right back."* Well, I love life, and life continues to love me right back!

SECTION 5

LIVING WITH ENTHUSIASM

CHAPTER 28

Life isn't about waiting for the rain to pass; it's about learning to dance in the rain.

—Unknown

Balinese philosophy is that all things are connected, whether they are animate or inanimate. It is called the principle of participation. There are two forces everywhere, positive and negative. Negative will never disappear. The macro-cosmos, or the universe, is made up of three parts: negative, which is the place of the demons; neutral, which belongs to humans; and the highest, where the gods reside, which is the most sacred. Humans must behave in an appropriate manner that will allow the positive order, or dharma, to take over the negative dharma. Everyone in their own way contributes to the dharma. It is necessary for everyone to work on maintaining balance deep within themselves. The sum of every action or karma is decisive for passage to the beyond. Karma represents every action that we have as humans, coming back to us eventually in one way or another.

June to September is a windy season in Bali. It isn't just the children that enjoy playing with kites. The fathers build huge kites that are sometimes five meters wide and have tails that can extend ten meters. It becomes a team effort to fly them! There is even a special whistle to call the wind. Every year, there is a big competition in Senur, and many villages participate. We were able to see one of these competitions, and it was quite spectacular! There were kites of all colors, shapes, and sizes flowing in the wind. I related it to my life, a reminder to me to flow with life as those kites were flowing in the wind that day.

Looking back, I realize more than ever how everything has purpose; life flows with people and experiences. Our lives intertwine with one another, and with every new experience we gain insight and strength. Doors open and they close; we deserve to walk through those doors. There is an element of risk to live your dreams. Life is an adventure, and through choices that I have made has come my reality at this moment. My choices have created my world, my perspective, and my character, who I am, and who I am becoming. I am what I am. Gratitude for the insight I have gained from experiences to this point of my life! Gratitude for the enthusiasm I have had for life and everything that it offers!

I can see how I was so blessed to have the opportunity of becoming a Celine Dion tribute artist, and the courage to walk through that door! This opportunity came into my life at a time of great sorrow, after the loss of my two sons and a thirty-year marriage that was unfulfilling. I wanted to fill that void with positive things. As a tribute artist for twelve years, traveling nationwide, meeting great people, I had some amazing experiences! After settling into my new life in Hawaii, I found new friends and exciting things to fill my time. The passion for pursuing my music is on hold just for now. I have been given this time to write this book, focus on my new relationship, and do the things that I want to do. After a lifetime of serving my church, community, and family, and working full-time, this is my time! So, here I am with the man of my dreams and the love of my life, sharing the time together in Bali. It is an amazing dream that has come true!

Through my own life's experiences, I have formed the belief that we each have the opportunity to come to this physical existence to learn. To learn the true power that each of us has to create whatever we want in life. Look at where you are at this very moment in time, and realize that your reality today is a result of all the previous thoughts that you have had, words that you have spoken, feelings that you have had, and choices that you have made. We are 100 percent responsible for our lives, and what we create is so empowering and so freeing!

> *There can be only one solution to any problem: a change in attitude and consciousness.*
> —*Greg Braden*

Attitude is everything! Attitude toward life changes everything in one direction or the other. You are not what happened to you, you are what you choose to become. You have choices each and every day.

> *I choose to feel enthusiasm for life.*
> *I choose to feel blessed.*
> *I choose to put a smile on my face.*
> *I choose to do what it takes to be healthy, mind, body, and spirit.*
> *I choose to have a great attitude.*
> *I choose to serve my fellow humans.*
> *I choose abundance.*
> *I choose to be happy.*

You choose! I am thankful for parents that were such great examples of having a positive attitude.

> *Do not let the behavior of others destroy your inner*
> *peace.*
> —*Dalai Lama*

My sweet husband, Mark, always says, "There are no problems, only opportunities for creative solutions." He is a great example of that principle!

CHAPTER 29

They who have conquered doubt and fear, have
conquered failure.

—James Allen

There is an abundance of flowers everywhere you go in Bali.
They are used for their offerings to the gods to show gratitude,
and also for prayer, since they represent purity and sincerity.
The lotus is very sacred, with its eight petals in the image of
the universe. The beautiful red hibiscus flowers represent the
warriors' courage. They would go off to battle with these big
bright flowers behind their ears. Each of us has the opportunity
to blossom like a flower as we overcome doubt and fear, growing
in experience and learning, in mind, body, and spirit.

Courage is to face anything that comes your way. There are only
two true emotions, love and fear. Every other emotion comes
from one of those two. Fear is taught to us at an early stage. We
learn fear either from our own experiences or from what we are
told by parents, family, friends, society, and church leaders. When
you have true unconditional love for yourself and for others, fear
is much easier to conquer. Fear is part of the human experience.
There is nothing wrong with having fears, but the most important
thing is to learn how to overcome those fears. It's not easy, and

often we don't even recognize our emotions coming from fear. Stop and think whenever you are reacting to a situation, *is my response coming from love or fear?* You have your own answer in your own heart. Fear holds you back! Marianne Williamson, a noted teacher and author, has observed, "Fear warps us, it stunts us, and it makes us neurotic." Instead of being afraid of the worst that can happen, focus on creating the best! You can create your own experience of any situation; you don't have to base your understanding of something on someone else's experience! To leave our comfort zone, to live fearlessly, believing we are protected with our angels by our sides, gives us unlimited freedom. Embrace the moment! Embrace the opportunity to try something new. Life begins just outside of your comfort zone. Be open to new experiences, for it is those experiences that give you insight. We cannot know how things truly are until we experience them. That is all we truly do know, nothing else. We all tend to judge things from our level of insight, from the personal experiences that we have had. To take personal responsibility for our choices and that which we have created takes courage.

> *When you think everything is someone else's fault, you will suffer a lot. When you realize that everything springs from yourself, you will learn both peace and joy.*
>
> *—Dali Lama*

If we create chaos, drama, or even what some people would consider hell on earth in our lives, then we learn from it and create ourselves out of it!

> *Nothing ever goes away until it teaches us what we need to know.*
>
> *—Pema Chodron*

Have the courage to be accountable. Do not become a victim. Do not blame anyone or anything for what you have attracted into your life. Learn from it, release it, and move forward as a more insightful person for your future. You were given this life because you are strong enough to live it. Live it courageously!

Gratitude is the key to abundance flowing into your life! When I lost my first son, my mother said to me, "Now is the time to focus on what you do have, not what you don't." That was one of the greatest lessons for me, and I have seen the wisdom in that statement many times in my life. I have an acquaintance that had a rough time accepting responsibility for what she has created in her life. She is always expecting more from others than they give and seems to be continually disappointed when people don't show up the way that she feels they should for her. Once in conversation, she was saying how rich people are so selfish and don't give enough. She had gone to a food bank in an upper-class community sponsored by a prominent women's organization to get groceries. Her words were, "These people gave me two bags full of just bread and canned goods. Those women should be giving us fresh fruits and veggies! They are so selfish!" It caught my attention because I feel it is becoming a more common mentality of taking all that you can, and expecting more and more. I felt that she lacked gratitude for that which was provided by individuals who truly believed that they were doing their part to serve their fellow humans. Changing your thoughts to gratitude will open up that abundance that is for all of us to have. The more you are thankful, the more you attract things to be thankful for!

Make a list of five things that you are thankful for before you go to bed every night. Focus on what you *do* have, not on what you *don't* have! Be aware of the things that people do for you, and pay it forward to others in your own life. Notice all the wonderful things that come into your life continually, and the abundance will continue to flow.

I was raised with the teaching of prayer and how powerful it is. Most people use prayer only when they want something, but I realize that prayer is an opportunity for gratitude! I believe in the power of prayer, how it can change you and how you look at life. When your heart is full of gratitude, there really isn't much room for anything else. I express gratitude every morning before my feet touch the floor and throughout the day as I take in the awesomeness of what life has to offer. Be aware and conscious of your surroundings and allow all your senses to come alive! You will be amazed at the wonderful things we can miss by not being aware.

> *Gratitude is the most single important ingredient to living a successful and fulfilled life.*
> —Jack Canfield

When you think about it, there are thousands of things to be grateful for! Acknowledge it. Verbalize it. Shout it out! Focus on all that you do have, not on what you don't have. The secret to having it all means believing that you already do! *Gratitude, gratitude, gratitude!*

Every one of us longs to feel loved, appreciated, and recognized. If we don't get that from where we are and who we are associating with, we go to where we do get it. If we could only be more aware of this and not hesitate to tell others how thankful we are that they came into our lives. Even those that challenge us have purpose in our lives. Be thankful for what they teach you. When you are associating with people, from my experience, if you come from a place of gratitude, their response to you will be more positive in most situations. How they react is about them and their perspective of themselves and life. It's about them, not about you, but you can always choose to react from a place of gratitude.

> *Feeling gratitude and not expressing it, is like wrapping a present and not giving it away.*
> —William Arthur Ward

Every thought, word, and deed has an effect on our physical bodies, and how we treat our physical bodies affects our thoughts and attitude! Our physical bodies are the "vehicles" that take us through life. How many of us have had a "dream car"? Maybe we have worked very hard to earn this beautiful car. We wash it, polish it, make sure that we get the oil changed regularly, and put good fuel into it. Taking care of this car is important so that this vehicle will serve us for a long time. Could we relate this to our physical bodies? What about our pets? Maybe we have a wonderful pet that we are blessed to nurture and serve, and we receive its unconditional love and companionship. We treasure pets and want them to stay healthy, so we feed them the very best food available. We cannot feed them cola, coffee, bagels, and doughnuts every day and then expect them to stay healthy. Sometimes we treat our material things and our animals better than we do our own selves.

We are physical beings, and that means physical laws apply. Follow those laws, and you will be blessed with vibrant health! The quality of life is more important than living a long time and not feeling well. Eating well, making healthy choices, exercising, staying active, and most importantly, having ageless thoughts by keeping your dreams alive is the closest thing that you will find to the "fountain of youth."

> *A man is not old until regrets take the place of dreams.*
>
> *—John Barrymore*

I think that we came to this earth with certain destinies, and we get to choose the journeys we take. Regarding wellness, we can choose to go through our journeys feeling great, with high energy, positive attitudes, and being productive; or we can choose the opposite—low energy, bad health, negative attitudes. If we choose to function from that place of discipline, high energy, courage, gratitude, and self-love in every thought, word, and deed, we will attract all those wonderful people and situations that function at that same place energetically into our lives. If we are functioning at low energy, with negative attitudes, being fearful and resigning ourselves to being victims, we will attract those people and situations into our lives. That is according to law of attraction. To be healthy physically, it will directly affect our mental outlook and our spiritual development.

I believe so strongly from my own past experiences that the mind, emotions, and feelings are the basis for most physical ailments! Looking back, in August 2009, Boyd, my former husband, called to tell me that he was engaged. Though we had a nice talk and I was so happy for him, I had quite a physical/emotional experience. I am sharing it because it was one example to me of how our emotions and feelings affect our physical health. My lower back had been bothering me for several years. I went to chiropractic care regularly and did my own preventative stretching. I had been told that it was an old injury that had just tightened up. It didn't affect my lifestyle too much, but it was definitely there and never went away, no matter what I did. While I was sitting on the couch talking to Boyd that day, the pain became excruciating, I couldn't move! In the study of psychoneuroimmunology, the sacral area of the back represents "not releasing." I began my positive affirmations to release the past: "I am the power and authority in my life, I release the past, and I claim my good now! I release Boyd; may God bless him in his new life. I honor the past, live the present, create the future. As I repeated these statements in my mind over and over, the pain gradually began to leave. By the time I was off the phone with Boyd, the pain was completely gone and has never returned! My back felt better than ever, and I felt a weight lift off of me. I felt freed and could move forward in my life with Mark, without looking back. Gratitude, gratitude, gratitude!

I was always amazed at the insight and wisdom of the Tibetan monks. The one thing that I recall the most is the teaching "The physical body *always* follows the mind and spirit." That was powerful to me because of the anxiety attacks that I had been experiencing after I lost my boys. I realized that I could change my thoughts and overcome my attacks, and I did, but it took discipline. I also learned that the lack of forgiveness on all levels, not forgiving ourselves and others, is a foundation for disease. It only hurts us when we harbor unforgiving feelings. I would say to love yourself enough to forgive yourself and love others enough to forgive them. We cannot control what others think, say, or do, but we can control what we think, say, or do! It takes learning to discipline yourself regarding the choices that you make. You are creating your reality for the future through your choices today.

We have five senses, and with those five senses we take in our surroundings. What we see, hear, touch, smell, and taste become part of us. It helps to design who we are. It is through our feelings that we create memories. If you look at a picture of the magnificent mountains, unless you were there and felt all your senses come alive, you activate only the visual. When you feel something, it internalizes that experience, which creates a memory. Choose wisely what you fill your five senses with. Love yourself enough to fill your senses with anything good, beautiful, and positive. There are so many wonderful books, movies, music, and so forth to uplift your mind, body, and spirit. Don't waste time with anything less.

From what I've observed, human beings are happiest when they are tapping into their creative sources. I'm sure that when we were born, there were spaces created for us to discover our talents and share them to contribute to the evolution of mankind in that moment. Discovering our talents and who we are is a process. We get to look at who we are with self-love and acceptance, looking deep into our own hearts. See who you really are, embracing and loving every part of that which you have been blessed with. We all have talents, probably more talents than we could ever imagine, but we put a cap on ourselves and tell ourselves, "Oh, I could never do that." All along you can do anything you want! You can at least try it. You might surprise yourself. If you find the passion for it, let that passion drive you. You can create it, ignite it! Find your talents and share them. Once you discover yourself, you have the freedom to share, to serve, to inspire, and to create.

I embrace that which is coming next in my life. I move forward with enthusiasm and courage. I stay open to all possibilities. I look for places to inspire and serve. I am forgiving and unconditionally loving.

I desire to be remembered as a woman who loved life and people. A woman filled with gratitude and appreciation, a woman that made a difference in the world even if in just a small way and a woman who had the courage to overcome fear not allowing fear to overcome her. A woman who embraced the moment!

I haven't a clue how my story will end, but that's all right. When you set out on a journey and night covers the road, that's when you discover the stars.

—Nancy Willard

Here's to creating the future!

Honor the Past, Release It, Live the Present, Embrace It, Create the Future, Ignite It!

—Bonnie Lee Mahler